Christina La
Clive Oxenden
Jerry Lambert
with Jane Hudson

ENGLISH FILE

Advanced Workbook with key

OXFORD
UNIVERSITY PRESS

Paul Seligson and Clive Oxenden are the original co-authors of
English File 1 and *English File 2*

Contents

STUDY LINK iChecker

Audio: when you see this symbol **iChecker**, go to the iTutor disc in the back of your Student's Book. Load the disc in your computer.

1

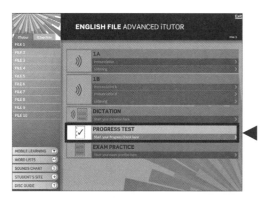

Choose the 'iChecker' tab at the top left of the screen.

2

Choose the File. Then select the audio track from lesson A or B.

You can transfer audio to a mobile device, e.g. your iPod, from the 'mobile learning' folder on the disc.

File test: At the end of every File, there is a test. To do the test, select 'Test' from the 'File' menu.

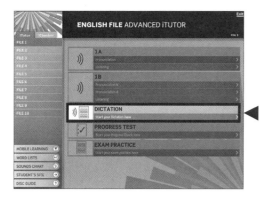

Dictation: At the end of every File, there is a dictation exercise. To do the dictation, select 'Dictation' from the 'File' menu.

Exam practice: At the end of every File, there is an exam practice exercise. To do the exercise, select 'Exam practice' from the 'File' menu.

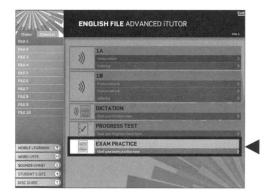

There is also more practice available on the English File website: www.oup.com/elt/englishfile

---

The other night I ate at a real nice family restaurant.
Every table had an argument going.

George Carlin, American comedian

1A Self-portrait

1 GRAMMAR *have*: auxiliary or main verb?

a Circle the correct words or phrases. In some sentences two answers are correct.

1 Some friends of ours had / had got / have had a nasty car accident last night.

2 She can't call her husband because she *doesn't have* / *hasn't* / *hasn't got* her mobile.

3 *Did you have* / *Had you* / *Have you got* a good time at your nephew's wedding?

4 Why are you going to be late? *Have you* / *Do you have* / *Have you got* to go to the doctor's?

5 We *had* / *had got* / *have got* our TV repaired last week, but it still doesn't work.

6 If she *had* / *have* / *had had* a coffee, she wouldn't have fallen asleep in the meeting!

7 I *didn't have to* / *hadn't got to* / *hadn't to* wear a uniform when I went to school.

8 The boss *didn't have* / *hadn't* / *won't have* heard the news yet because he's been off sick.

b Complete the sentences with the correct form of *have*. Sometimes more than one answer is possible.

1 They couldn't go to the concert because they _didn't have_ tickets.

2 Jessica doesn't need a company car because she _____ travel for her job.

3 This is a great car, Alex. How long _____ you _____ it?

4 Let's take a taxi. We _____ time to walk.

5 I can't lend you my bike. I _____ it repaired at the moment.

6 Ben doesn't know everyone yet. He _____ working in our office for very long.

7 Welcome to the UK. _____ you _____ a good flight?

8 I'll give you a lift. What time _____ you _____ to be at the airport?

2 VOCABULARY personality

a Circle the correct word.

1 Emily doesn't need any help – she's very *conscientious* / *gentle* / self-sufficient.

2 I don't like my boss much. He can be very *bright* / *sarcastic* / *steady*.

3 She's a really *conscientious* / *spontaneous* / *sympathetic* student, so she attends all her lectures.

4 My father is great at household repairs because he's very *resourceful* / *sarcastic* / *straightforward*.

5 The doctor was quite *self-sufficient* / *spontaneous* / *thorough* and examined the patient carefully.

6 I had a terrible day at work, but my husband wasn't very *determined* / *steady* / *sympathetic*.

7 My grandmother was a *bright* / *gentle* / *thorough* woman who was kind to everyone.

8 My best friend is very *determined* / *resourceful* / *straightforward*; there's nothing complicated about her.

b Complete the verbs in the sentences.

1 Ann's very indecisive. She's always **ch**_anging_ her mind.

2 On the surface, she **s**_____ not to care, but deep down I'm sure she's terribly upset.

3 He's so innocent, he often gets **t**_____ advantage of.

4 She's very spontaneous, but her boyfriend **t**_____ to plan ahead.

5 We agreed to some of their demands, but they still **r**_____ to compromise.

6 I'm not adventurous, so I don't **t**_____ risks.

c Replace the words in **bold** with a personality idiom using the word in brackets.

1 My aunt can be a bit impatient, but she's got **a very kind personality**. (heart) _a heart of gold_

2 That customer is **really annoying** – he's always calling to complain. (neck) _____

3 My friend's dad **gets angry very easily**, so we try to keep out of his way. (quick) _____

4 Our new neighbour is **very reserved and unfriendly**. (fish) _____

5 My parents are very **sensible and practical**. They're full of good advice. (earth) _____

6 My brother is **very easily persuaded**. I can get him to do whatever I want. (soft) _____

3 PRONUNCIATION using a dictionary

a Underline the stressed syllable in the words below.

1 straight|<u>for</u>|ward
2 con|sci|en|tious
3 cu|ri|ous
4 de|ter|mined
5 gen|tle
6 self-|suf|fi|cient
7 stea|dy
8 re|source|ful
9 sar|cas|tic
10 spon|ta|ne|ous
11 sym|pa|the|tic
12 tho|rough

b **iChecker** Listen and check. Practise saying the words.

4 LEXIS IN CONTEXT
What's your personality?

Look at the Lexis in Context on Student's Book p.6. Then complete the sentences.

1 We followed your directions **to the l***etter*___, so we didn't get lost.
2 Maria **got st**_____ on a question, so she couldn't finish her homework.
3 It's best to **put t**_____ a list of points for discussion before you hold a meeting.
4 The jacket in the window **caught my e**_____, so I went into the shop to try it on.
5 It wasn't easy to **go r**_____ the exhibition because there were so many people.
6 The gambler went with his **g**_____ **feeling** and put all his money on the same horse.
7 A good manager faces problems **h**_____ **on** in order to solve them as quickly as possible.
8 My flatmate always **puts o**_____ doing the washing up until there aren't any clean plates left.
9 I didn't want to hurt my sister's feelings, so I told her a **wh**_____ **lie** about her new dress.

5 LISTENING

a **iChecker** Listen to four people comparing having brothers and sisters and being an only child. Do they mention more advantages or disadvantages of having siblings?

b Listen again. Which speaker mentions these advantages of having brothers and sisters?

A ☐ learning to interact with other children
B ☐ not being spoilt
C ☐ not being the sole centre of your parents' expectations
D ☐ being able to share the responsibility of caring for elderly parents

c Listen again with the audio script on p.69 and try to guess the meaning of any words that you don't know. Then check in your dictionary.

6 READING

a Read the article once and choose the sentence that best describes Ang Lee.

1 He is more content now than he was as a child.
2 He is as content now as he was as a child.
3 He was more content as a child than he is now.

b Read the text again and choose a, b, c, or d.

1 How did Ang Lee regard his father as a child?
   a He admired him.
   b He was fond of him.
   c He was in awe of him.
   d He hated him.

2 What is Ang Lee's greatest criticism of his father?
   a He had too many children.
   b He lacked a sense of humour.
   c He forced his children to study art.
   d He never took them to the cinema.

3 What was Sheng Lee's opinion of his son's choice of career?
   a He had no faith in Ang's ability to make films.
   b He hoped that Ang would be successful.
   c He regarded it as a respectable profession.
   d He didn't think it was a proper job.

4 What does Ang Lee say about his mother?
   a She brought up her children well.
   b She was a soft touch.
   c She should have been more rebellious.
   d She stood out from all his friends' mothers.

5 Why didn't Ang Lee do very well at school?
   a Because he wasn't very bright.
   b Because he never did his homework.
   c Because he didn't focus on what he had to study.
   d Because he often played truant.

6 Why were the first years of Ang Lee's marriage difficult?
   a Because his wife didn't approve of his career choice.
   b Because he didn't have any paid employment.
   c Because he had been brought up in a different way from his wife.
   d Because his children needed special attention.

c Look at the highlighted adjectives. What do you think they mean? Check in your dictionary.

> **Glossary**
>
> **tiger mother** a demanding mother who pushes her children to high levels of achievement

Ang Lee: my family values

The film director on moving out of his father's shadow and being determined to make life fun for his own children.

My late father, Sheng Lee, was a traditional Chinese authority figure. He represented the traditional Chinese patriarchal society. I was always living in his shadow; that was my big thing. I was shy and docile and never rebellious. But he taught me how to survive and how to be useful. He was a very pragmatic man, the headmaster of a high school – I don't know if that was a good or a bad thing.

When I was growing up [as one of four children] he made me study all the time; studying was all that was important to him. He was not much fun and he was kind of disappointed with me in some ways. Artistically, I was very repressed. I never really got to express myself and wasn't exposed to much art other than watching movies once a week.

My father wanted me to have a respectable profession. Teaching was respectable to him. He said, 'Get a degree and teach in university.' When I wasn't working he would say, 'What are you going to do? Are you going to set an example for your kids?' But I just wanted to make movies, so I never fulfilled the hopes he had for me. Even when I was successful, he would say, 'Now it's time to do something real.'

My mother, Se-Tsung, was very submissive with my father and obedient. I don't have many issues with her: she was a very good mother to me and my siblings. When I was growing up, women didn't matter as much. It was patriarchal, all about the father. Everyone tried to please my father.

As a kid I could not really concentrate on books or homework. I did OK to poorly at school because I would fantasize all the time, having a lot of fun in my head because I didn't have a lot of fun. It took 35 years to release all that energy. I was repressed and then that repression was released when I became a filmmaker.

When I had my own family I was different because I didn't want to do that to my own kids, so I am fun. My wife [Jane Lin, a microbiologist] is the tiger mother in the home, the wise one in the family. I am like the third kid at home. She makes all the rules. We [our two sons, Mason, an actor, and Haan, an artist] obey. Before I got work as a director, my wife worked. I was lucky, my wife provided for the family herself and never asked me to find a job. I was picking up the kids from school and doing the cooking and writing. Most of the time I didn't do anything – there was a lot of anxiety because I couldn't invest in anything apart from filmmaking.

A professional is one who does his best work
when he feels the least like working.
Frank Lloyd Wright, American architect

1B Nice work!

1 LEXIS IN CONTEXT
What I'm really thinking

Look at the Lexis in Context on Student's Book p.8.
Then complete the expressions.

1 I wouldn't worry about the interview – it's not a matter
of l*ife or death*.
2 Turn that music off! It's **doing my h** *ead* **in**.
3 If you paid attention, you might be able to **k** *eep*
up with the lesson.
4 My father is an intellectual snob. He l *ooks* **down**
on people who haven't been to university.
5 My mind's **gone bl** *ank*! I can't remember my own
phone number!
6 The traffic begins to **b** *uild* **up** at around 7 o'clock
on weekdays.
7 It **breaks my h** *eart* when I see pictures of
malnourished children on the TV.
8 I don't mind dealing with the public, but it **gets**
w *earing* answering the same questions all day.

2 VOCABULARY work

a **Circle** the correct word.

1 My company offers considerable benefits to the
colleagues | co-workers | **staff.**
2 It's so *repetitive | challenging | rewarding* when you see
your students really start to improve.
3 My girlfriend's job is quite *rewarding | demanding |*
tedious, so she gets very stressed.
4 I'm hoping to get *a rise | promoted | raised* to Head of
Department by the end of the year.
5 He wants to *quit | employ | resign* a new assistant to deal
with his mail.
6 Over 2,000 workers will be *fired | made redundant |*
sacked when the car factory closes down.
7 Working on a production line can be *challenging |*
motivating | monotonous because you do the same thing
all day every day.
8 My husband is *off work | out of work | laid off* with a bad
back at the moment.
9 I'm really jealous of my sister because she gets so many
skills | qualifications | perks in her job.
10 We're looking to *hire | fire | lay off* somebody with a
positive, can-do attitude.

b Match the words in **A** to the words in **B** and complete
the sentences below.

A	academic	apply for	career	clocking
	events	full	job	permanent	~~work~~

B	contract	~~experience~~	hunting	ladder
	management	off	a position	qualifications	time

1 The company is offering *work experience* to
students in their final year of school.
2 Looking after small children is a
_____-_____ occupation.
3 I've spent six months _____-_____,
but I'm still out of work.
4 She never went to university so she doesn't have many
_____ _____ .
5 He's very ambitious, so he's hoping to climb the
_____ _____ as quickly as possible.
6 If you're good at organizing parties, you could work
in _____ _____ .
7 I'm hoping they'll give me a _____ _____
when I finish my three-month trial period.
8 She cleared her desk and locked the drawers before
_____ _____ .
9 I'm going to _____ _____ _____
_____ as a sales assistant at the new shopping
centre, which is opening soon.

3 GRAMMAR discourse markers (1): linkers

a ~~Cross out~~ the linker that is NOT possible in the sentences.

1 We set off at dawn ~~owing to~~ *| in order to | so as to* avoid
the rush-hour traffic.
2 Laila's mother-in-law was a very difficult woman.
However | Nevertheless | Consequently Laila couldn't
help liking her.
3 *In spite of | Even though | Despite* being the better
player, Richard lost the match.
4 Sales figures have fallen drastically *due to | because |*
owing to the recession.
5 The workers covered the furniture with sheets *so as not*
to | not to | in order not to splash it with paint.
6 After his accident, my brother sold his car *as | since |*
due to he couldn't afford the insurance.
7 We accept full responsibility for the error and *nevertheless |*
consequently | therefore wish to offer you a full refund.
8 I agreed to help *although | in case | even though* I didn't
feel like it.

b Rewrite the sentences using the word(s) in brackets.

1 We have not received payment for your last bill. Consequently, you are being sent a reminder. (since)
   You are being sent a reminder *since we have not received payment for your last bill* .

2 She wrote down the appointment so that she wouldn't forget the time. (so as)
   She wrote down the appointment _____
   _____ .

3 The motorway is being resurfaced and so it will be closed until further notice. (result)
   The motorway is being resurfaced, and _____
   _____ .

4 The flight is delayed because the incoming plane arrived late. (due)
   The flight is delayed _____
   _____ .

5 He decided to apply for the job although he didn't meet all the requirements. (despite)
   He decided to apply for the job _____
   _____ .

6 They had an early night in order to be ready for the exam the next day. (so that)
   They had an early night _____
   _____ .

7 She was offered a job even though she wasn't able to go to the interview. (spite)
   She was offered the job _____
   _____ .

8 He was unable to attend the conference because he was ill. (owing)
   He was unable to attend the conference _____
   _____ .

4 LEXIS IN CONTEXT Skyscanner

Look at the Lexis in Context on Student's Book p.11. Then complete the sentences.

1 When you live near an airport, the noise of the planes eventually becomes the **n** *orm* .
2 Her sickness was just a **pl**_____ so she could stay at home.
3 Please don't let the fact that I got the promotion over you become an **i**_____ between us.
4 He wanted a job that was **tr**_____-**f**_____ , so he became a flight attendant.
5 I can handle a fairly heavy **w**_____ . I'm used to doing lots of things at once.
6 How do we **t**_____ the problem of unemployment?

5 PRONUNCIATION word stress

a Underline the stressed syllable in the words below.

1 re|war|ding
2 free|lance
3 tem|po|ra|ry
4 vo|lun|tary
5 com|pas|sio|nate
6 ma|ter|ni|ty
7 per|ma|nent
8 mo|ti|va|ting
9 mo|no|to|nous
10 a|ca|de|mic
11 ma|nage|ment
12 qua|li|fi|ca|tions

b **iChecker** Listen and check. Practise saying the words.

c Circle the word with a different sound.

1	tree	tedious	colleague	event
2	bike	quit	resign	fire
3	ear	career	perks	experience
4	fish	redundant	demanding	benefits

d **iChecker** Listen and check. Practise saying the words.

6 READING

a Read the article once. How would the writer answer the question in the title?

'BEST JOB IN THE WORLD': FACT OR FICTION?

Who wouldn't jump at the chance of 'working' for six months as the caretaker of an idyllic holiday island off the coast of Queensland, Australia? For Ben Southall, winner of the 'Best Job in the World' contest, the prospect seemed like a dream come true. The 34-year-old former charity worker, from Petersfield, UK, beat 34,000 other competitors for the job, which also came with a £2.5 million beachside mansion boasting magnificent ocean views. ¹_____

Alas, at the end of his posting, Mr Southall admitted that being a tourist ambassador for paradise was not all plain sailing. In fact, there was very little time for sailing at all – or sunbathing, or simply relaxing and enjoying those fine ocean views.

²_____ 'It has been very busy, busier than most people would have imagined, and certainly busier than I had imagined,' Mr Southall told the press, adding that he had been 'too busy' to sit back and reflect on it all very much. ³_____

True, somewhere along the line he did also learn to sail, play golf, and kayak. But even those activities were limited by the need to keep a running web commentary about what he was up to. He posted more than 75,000 words in 60 separate blogs – the equivalent of a small novel – uploaded more than 2,000 photos, and 'tweeted more than 730 times,' according to Peter Lawlor, Queensland's Tourism Minister.

⁴_____ Readers of the website complained that the jam-packed itineraries organized by Tourism Queensland left Mr Southall no time to explore the reef privately and deliver detailed accounts of his experiences. They also said that the blogs were too sanitized and promotional, without any critical or personal angle.

⁵_____ Nevertheless, in what is perhaps the ultimate proof of his new skills as a PR man, he still insists he enjoyed himself thoroughly. And his demanding taskmasters at Tourism Queensland are also pleased, so much so that they have offered him a new 18-month, six-figure contract to promote their state worldwide.

In his spare time, if he gets any, he will also start on a book about his experiences over the last six months. Whether it will prove a best-selling beachside read is another matter.

b Five sentences and paragraphs have been removed from the article. Read it again and match A–F to the gaps 1–5. There is one sentence or paragraph you do not need to use.

A Indeed, in the view of his online audience, he spent so much time blogging about having a good time that he didn't really have much of a time at all.

B Instead, he found himself working seven days a week, slave to a gruelling schedule of promotional events, press conferences, and administration.

C Soon after he started, Ben had a brush with death after being stung by a jellyfish. The incident did not deter him, however, and he got on with his job.

D Either way, Mr Southall admits that he is now tired out – and in need of a holiday. 'It was a job that needed 18 to 19 hours' work every day,' he said. 'Not just the interviews and the social side of it, but also blogging and uploading pictures – it's very time consuming.'

E Other perks in the contest included a £74,000 salary, a private pool, and a courtesy golf buggy.

F A snapshot of just how demanding the Best Job in the World could be is provided by Tourism Queensland's official report on Mr Southall's posting. It announced that he had visited 90 'exotic locations', made 47 video diaries, and given more than 250 media interviews.

c Look at the highlighted idioms and match them to the definitions.

1 very full _____
2 at some point during an activity _____
3 simple and free from trouble _____
4 was doing _____
5 is very different _____
6 accept an opportunity with enthusiasm

_____

7 LISTENING

a (iChecker) Listen to a man talking about a kind of job he would love to do and one he would hate. What are the jobs?

b Listen again. Answer the questions.

1 Why does the man think he would be good at the first job?
2 What does he think might be the downside?
3 Why does he think he would hate the second job?
4 Has he done this kind of work? If so, did he like it?

c Listen again with the audio script on p.69 and try to guess the meaning of any words that you don't know. Then check in your dictionary.

1 LOOKING AT LANGUAGE
discourse markers

Complete the sentences with a discourse marker from the list.

anyway	apparently	as to	basically
I mean	in a way	~~of course~~	really

1 My sister gets quite lonely in the evenings. _Of course_ her husband's around, but he's always falling asleep in front of the TV.
2 I can't remember much about my childhood. _____, I spent most of the time running wild with the other kids in the village. That's what my mum tells me, anyway.
3 My nephew's such a lovely boy. But _____ what he wants to do in the future, he hasn't got a clue.
4 We've had a great holiday but _____, I'm glad to be going home. I've missed the cat!
5 If I have to take my daughter to work, I _____ do the same as I would on a normal day.
6 That woman isn't _____ her mother; she's her stepmother.
7 I'm hoping to move out soon. _____, I love my parents, but I'd like a place of my own.
8 I'm not going to apply for that job. It's too far away and _____, the pay is too low.

2 READING

a Read the article. Five sentences have been removed from it. Match the sentences A–F to the gaps 1–5. There is one sentence you do not need to use.

A This gives them the chance to learn from each others' experiences, and also to reflect more profoundly on their own.

B The idea is that all daughters and sons should be able to participate.

C Each year, a theme is chosen for the event, and a new logo is designed for the T-shirts worn by participants.

D The success of the event is reflected in the well over twenty years in which it has been running.

E After that, they should spend the rest of the day shadowing their mother or father in all that they do.

F Too often, this led to them dropping out of school early.

b Underline five words or phrases you don't know. Use your dictionary to look up their meaning and pronunciation.

Take Our Daughters and Sons to Work Day

Many parents would probably agree that work and family life are not always easy to balance. Not so the 37 million US employees who take part each year in the *Take Our Daughters and Sons to Work Day*. On this day, the fourth Thursday in April, parents in over 3.5 million companies take their children into work to give them a taste of just what it is their parents get up to all day. [1]____ Today, it is now regarded as a kind of national institution.

The scheme has not always catered for both boys and girls. It was originally conceived in 1993 by the non-profit organization *Ms. Foundation for Women* as the *Take Our Daughters to Work Day*. In the early 1990s, research had revealed that schoolgirls were often lacking the confidence they needed to succeed. [2]____ It was hoped that the event would show them the importance of finishing their education and what they could achieve if they did so. By 2003, it had become apparent that boys were suffering a similar lack of self-esteem, and so they were also incorporated into the scheme, which changed its name accordingly.

The *Take Our Daughters and Sons to Work Day* takes place on a school day, because it is a valuable educational experience. In class the next day, pupils are expected to share news from their day at the office with their classmates. [3]____ Older students taking part in the scheme, aimed primarily at eight- to 18-year-olds, can get a good idea of the attitude and behaviour common to the workplace, which helps prepare them for any part-time jobs they might do in the future.

Parents are encouraged to enhance their child's experience by preparing carefully for the day beforehand. The organizers recommend discussing the day before and after the child is brought to work so that they get as much as possible out of their visit. According to employees who have already taken part in the programme, children should be introduced to their parent's colleagues to get an insight into how the team works. [4]____ In some cases, companies plan special activities, which make the day more interactive and memorable for the children, and give parents a chance to catch up on any urgent work alone.

It is not only the children of employees that the scheme is aimed at, hence its name: *Take Our Daughters and Sons to Work*. [5]____ This means that workers may invite the children of friends, relatives, neighbours, or even children from residential homes to accompany them. The main aim is to expose as many schoolchildren as possible to the world of work in the hope that it will give them a goal in life to work towards and help them land their dream job.

2A Changing language

1 LEXIS IN CONTEXT Spell it out

Look at the Lexis in Context on Student's Book p.14. Then complete the sentences.

1 Today there is no **st**_igma___ attached to speaking with a regional accent.
2 Even today, languages are more **fl**_____ than we suppose.
3 Loan words have played as big a **p**_____ in English as they have in other European languages.
4 Students are sometimes bewildered by the **r**_____ nature of irregular verbs.
5 Most nationalities have an authority they look to for **g**_____ on correct grammar.

2 PRONUNCIATION
sound–spelling relationships

a Say the words aloud. Write **S** if the **bold** letters are pronounced the same or **D** if the pronunciation is different.

1 🐍 snake	2 🚲 bike	3 🐴 horse
sympathetic **s**ynonym	de**s**pite **s**ince	th**aw** j**aw**
_S_	_D_	____

4 🐦 bird	5 🧹 witch	6 🎷 jazz
b**ir**th f**ir**m	**wh**irl **wh**ose	**j**ealous **j**ournalist
____	____	____

7 🏠 house	8 chess	9 🐦 bird	10 ☎ phone
dis**h**onest in**h**erit	**ch**ime **ch**orus	w**or**m w**or**th	l**ow**er p**ow**er

b 🔲 iChecker Listen and check. Practise saying the words.

3 GRAMMAR pronouns

a Right (✔) or wrong (✗)? Correct the mistakes in the highlighted phrases.

1 One need to listen to both sides of the story in order to find out the truth.   ✗ _One needs to listen_____
2 Two of my friends aren't talking to themselves because they've had a big argument. _____
3 As soon as he woke up, Brad washed and dressed and left the house. _____
4 The receptionist accompanied us to the meeting room and said we should help us to tea and coffee.

_____
5 When a guest leaves his room, we recommend locking the door. _____
6 I much prefer travelling by my own.

_____
7 She felt dizzy when she looked out of the window and saw the land so far below herself. _____
8 This is a delicious cake. Did you make it yourself?

_____

b Complete the mini-dialogues with a suitable pronoun.

1 A Who hasn't handed in _their__ homework?
  B Me. Sorry. Here it is.
2 A What a gorgeous dress! Where did you get it?
  B Well, actually, I made it _myself_.
3 A Why isn't Judy with Pete tonight?
  B They're not going out with _____ any more.
4 A I think CD players are completely out of date.
  B Yes. _____ doesn't see many of them these days.
5 A I've just been promoted!
  B Well done! You must be really proud of _____!
6 A Why don't you join the army?
  B I don't know. _____ say it's really tough.
7 A Who's Grace going round Europe with?
  B No one. She's going by _____.
8 A People say _____ shouldn't sit in a draught.
  B Rubbish! There's nothing wrong with fresh air.

c Complete the text with *it* or *there*.

¹ *It*   takes me ages to get to work, although
²   's only a few miles from my house to the
office. ³   isn't too much traffic on the roads
when I leave home, but ⁴   's impossible to park
by the time I reach the city centre. ⁵   are always
loads of cars driving around looking for a space and these
days ⁶   are parking meters, so you have to pay.
⁷   used to be a company bus, but they stopped
it because ⁸   were only a few of us that used it.
⁹   's all right for those people with a motorbike,
but ¹⁰   's really tedious for us car drivers!

4 VOCABULARY learning languages

a (Circle) the correct word(s).

1 You have to *say* / *speak* / *talk* a number of languages to
be a flight attendant.
2 The speaker went too fast, so it was impossible to
pass for / *pick up* / *take in* all the information.
3 Bear in mind that children don't always *say* / *talk* / *tell*
the truth.
4 Did you manage to *brush up* / *get by* / *pick up* any
Portuguese while you were in Lisbon?
5 Sorry, I didn't get that. Can you *say* / *speak* / *tell*
it again, please?
6 How will you *pick up* / *get by* / *pass for* in Kyoto if you
don't speak any Japanese?
7 He wants to have a few days off, so he needs to *say* / *talk*
/ *tell* to his boss.
8 She needs to *brush up* / *pick up* / *take in* her French
before she takes up her new job in Paris.

b Replace the **bold** words in sentences 1–5 with a more
formal word or expression.

1 Students will be tested on **vocabulary** and grammar
in this part of the test. *lexis*
2 Candidates are **asked** to switch off their mobile
phones before the exam. r
3 A serious **mistake** has been found in the manuscript.
e
4 This is an automatically generated email. Please do not
attempt to **answer** it. r
5 Children brought up in a bilingual environment may
have more than one native **language**. t

c Complete the sentences with an idiom containing the
word in brackets.

1 She told me her name, but I can't _get my tongue round_
it. (tongue)
2 He got   and
thought Anna was being sarcastic when she was trying
to be nice. (stick)
3 Wait, give me a minute. Oh, it's
            , but I just can't think of the word! (tip)
4 I didn't mean that at all – I think we're talking
                        . (cross)
5 This instruction manual is so confusing. I can't
                        it. (head)

5 READING

a Read the article once. Which three features of a
language may cause it to affect our personality?
[handwritten: construction 2) culture 3) mesere... when... no... my]

b Read the text again and match the missing sentences
A–H to the gaps 1–6. There are two sentences you do
not need to use.

A French has an unusually large vocabulary, allowing the
speaker to find extremely precise words with specific
meanings.

B In Russian, however, the emphasis is on the shape,
not the material, so all of these would merely be 'little
glasses' or 'stakanchiki'.

C Speaking it will force you to think longer and harder, and
you may feel like you played a five-set tennis match after
a conversation.

D And yet, his personality seemed to vary.

E After the first ad, they referred to her with positive
words, such as ('self-sufficient' and ('strong', suggesting
that they looked up to her.

F A comparative analysis between languages shows that
languages may well rewire our minds.

G He and his mentor, Edward Sapir, compared this with
English and noticed how the two languages had a
completely different system for forming words.

H He claims that it is thoughts that lead to language, and
not the other way round.

c Look at the highlighted words and match them to a
neutral equivalent.

1 insulting *derogatory*
2 work out *formulate*
3 agree *concur*
4 against *versus*
5 decide *determine*
6 spoke to *addressed smb*
7 showing *revealing*

New language, new personality?

When Jacques was 12 years old, his mother began speaking to him only in French, his father addressed him only in Greek, and he was sent to an English-speaking day school in Paris. Of course, the child was the same person no matter which of the three languages he was using. ¹D 'I felt probably ruder and more aggressive in Greek, clear and concise in French, and creative and long-winded in English,' he said.

Jacques' experience of languages seems to concur with a theory developed back in 1931 in the linguistics department of Yale University. A student by the name of Benjamin Whorf was carrying out some research into the Algonquian language, Shawnee, which was spoken by only 200 people at the time. ²G Their findings led them to develop the 'Sapir-Whorf hypothesis' which claims that the language we speak shapes our experience of the world.

But how is it possible for a language to determine our understanding of the world and therefore affect our personality? The answer may lie in the way that different languages are constructed. In Greek, for example, the verb usually comes first, its conjugation revealing the tone and meaning of the rest of the sentence, making it easier for the listener to interrupt. ³F And in English, words tend to be more adaptable and easier to rhyme.

Yet construction of a language is not the only determining factor. A study at Baruch College, New York, suggests that culture may also play a part. Researchers showed a group of bilingual Hispanic-American women the same commercial about a woman doing housework, first in Spanish and then in English. ⁴E But when the women watched the English version, they used the derogatory terms 'traditional' and 'dependent'. Despite the striking contrast between the adjectives, it is not clear whether it was the language itself that influenced the volunteers' choices or the cultural habits associated with that language.

A third determining factor may be the way in which objects are classified in a language. Let's take Russian as an example. A Russian speaker learning English would associate 'glass' and 'cup' with their translations, 'stakan' and 'chashka'. Yet, in English we call all sorts of things 'cups': coffee to-go cups, Styrofoam™ cups, plastic cups, paper cups. ⁵B Therefore, in order for the Russian speaker to correctly learn English (or vice versa), he must pay attention to not just direct translations but also to categorizations, in this case shape versus material.

Although there seems to be a great deal of evidence supporting the argument that language influences personality, there are obviously those who do not agree. One of the greatest opponents is Stephen Pinker of Harvard University. ⁶A Consequently, he believes that as long as we can think about something, then we can formulate a way to say it. And so the debate rages on. But as Jacques himself points out: it makes a big difference which language to choose when it comes to discussing a subject like economics!

6 LISTENING

a You're going to listen to two people talking about their experiences of being non-native speakers of English. Before you listen, check the meaning of the words in the glossary.

> **Glossary**
>
> **Glasgow** a large city in Scotland
>
> **BBC English / Standard English** English as spoken with a 'standard' pronunciation which corresponds to the pronunciation given in a dictionary
>
> **General American** US English as spoken with a 'standard' pronunciation which corresponds to the pronunciation given in a dictionary
>
> **Scots** a way of speaking English found in Scotland
>
> **Geordie** a way of speaking English typically from the area in and around Newcastle, in the north-east of England
>
> **University of Michigan** a university in the mid-west of the USA
>
> **The Simpsons** a very well-known US cartoon series

b (iChecker) Listen once. What four questions do they answer?

1 _is it easier to underst non-native sp?_
2 _how do you feel about being corrected_
3 _embarrassing stories about misunderstanding_
4 _anything still difficult about Eng_

c Listen again and mark the sentences **W** (woman), **M** (man), or **B** (both).

1 They think that native speakers don't spell as well as some non-native speakers. _M_
2 They feel comfortable about being corrected. _B_
3 They usually get what non-native speakers say because there is no hidden meaning. _M_
4 They notice a gap in their knowledge of English because they were born elsewhere. _B_
5 They could have had an awkward conversation, but, thankfully, it never occurred. ___
6 They find some native speakers easier to understand than others. _M, W_

d Listen again with the audio script on p.69 and try to guess the meaning of any words that you don't know. Then check in your dictionary.

My childhood was endless –
from eight to 18 felt like hundreds of years.

Karl Lagerfeld, German designer

2B Do you remember...?

1 LEXIS IN CONTEXT *Boy*

Look at the Lexis in Context on Student's Book p.18.
Then complete the words.

1 When I was little, I used to **grab** my mother's hand if
we came across a big dog on the street.

2 At lunchtime, everybody would go **r** *ound* to the
canteen to be first in the queue.

3 Dinner would be **b** *oiling* **a**_____ in a pot
on the stove when we used to get home from school.

4 'Well done!' my father said, as he **sl** *apped* me on
the back for scoring the winning goal.

5 My mother was always **c** *oncockin* different kinds of
soup out of whatever she could find in the fridge.

6 I can still **p** *ict|ure* the first teacher I ever had – she
seemed ancient to me, but she was extremely kind.

7 When the bell rang, we would all **l** *eap* from
our seats before the teacher could set any homework.

2 GRAMMAR the past:
habitual events and specific incidents

a Right (✓) or wrong (✗)? Correct any mistakes in the
highlighted phrases.

1 As a child, Tom was always knocking off my glasses
when my parents weren't looking. ✓

2 My brother climbed a tree when he slipped and
fell. ✗ *was climbing*

3 My mum had been forgetting to turn off the oven, so
there was a terrible smell of gas in the kitchen. ✗
had forgotten

4 Most days we rode our bikes to school, but sometimes
we were catching the bus. ✗ *caught the bus*

5 One day, our car used to break down in the fast lane of
the motorway. ✗ *broke down*

6 When we were kids, our dad would give us a packed
lunch and send us out to play for the day. ✓
_____

7 Emily's grandparents would live in an old farmhouse in
the heart of the countryside. ✗ *grp. lived/used to liv*

8 I'd hidden in the bushes for over an hour before I
realized that everyone else had gone home. ✗
I had been hiding. before

9 When we got home from school that evening, our
parents still worked. ✗ *our p. were still workin*

10 I burst into tears when I saw what my brother had done
to my favourite doll. ✓ _____

b Complete the text with the correct form of the verbs
in brackets. Use a narrative tense or *would* / *used to*.

When I [1] *was* (be) little, I [2] *used to* (share) a bedroom
with my sister Catherine. As I was eight years her junior,
I obviously [3] *used to g* (go) to bed earlier than her.
As soon as I [4] *cleaned* (clean) my teeth, my mum
[5] *lay/would* (lie) on my sister's bed and sing me nursery
rhymes until I [6] *fell* (fall) asleep.

One night when my mum *had been staying* (sing) for about
five minutes, she suddenly [8] *stopped* (stop) and
[9] *stood up* (stand) up. I [10] *looked* (look) over at her
and saw that she [11] *was staring* (stare) at something on
the wall above my head. Without raising her voice, she
[12] *told* (tell) me to go downstairs where my dad
[13] *was watching* (watch) TV. Later she told me she [14] *had seen*
(see) a big, hairy spider climb out of the air grille and make its
way up the wall. I [15] *didn't* (not sleep) much that night,
as you can imagine!

3 VOCABULARY
word building: abstract nouns

a Complete the sentences with the abstract nouns of the **bold** words.

1 When my aunt **lost** her husband, she was driven to despair. She never got over her _loss_ .
2 I'm **afraid** of flying. I've never been abroad because of my _fear_ of crashing. _fright_
3 My dad's health has **improved** a lot. We've noticed a great _improvement_
4 We **hated** our physics teacher with a vengeance. I'm fairly sure our _hatred_ was returned as well.
5 The **dead** statesman was buried immediately. The whole country mourned his _death_ .
6 For medicine to work, you have to **believe** in it. It is often this _faith/belief_ that makes you well again.
7 Rosie was so **ashamed** of her behaviour that her face burned with _shame / embarrassment_

b Complete the sentences with the correct form of the words in brackets.

1 I am truly grateful to my cousin for her _friendship_ during these difficult times. (friend)
2 In some societies, the _wisdom_ of the older generation must never be questioned. (wise)
3 Despite a very traumatic _childhood_ , Adam grew up to be quite a sensible young man. (child)
4 Ruth tried to hide the _sadness_ in her eyes as she left the house for ever. (sad)
5 We had a big family _celebration_ for my dad's 80th birthday. (celebrate)
6 I remembered to renew my _membership_ at the golf club before the tournament started. (member)
7 My grandmother will be staying in a nursing home until she has fully recovered from her _illness_ . (ill)
8 We dread our history lectures because every week we nearly die of _boredom_ . (bored)

4 PRONUNCIATION
word stress with suffixes

a Look at the word pairs. Circle the abstract nouns where the stress is different.

1 compete — (competition)
2 neighbour — neighbourhood
3 partner — partnership
4 happy — happiness
5 celebrate — (celebration)
6 relation — relationship
7 imagine — (imagination)
8 believe — belief
9 curious — (curiosity)

b **iChecker** Listen and check. Practise saying the words.

5 LISTENING

a **iChecker** Listen to five people talking about their earliest memories. Which speaker doubts whether they can actually remember experiencing the incident? N4

b Listen again and answer the questions with speakers 1–5. Use each speaker twice. Who talks about…?

A [3] a significant day in many people's lives , _Wimbledon_
B [5] an everyday occurrence
C [4] a moment just before or after a flight
D [2] some dramatic weather
E [5] finding something beautiful
F [1] something that others may find quite boring
G [3] receiving advice from a parent
H [4] seeing a photo of themselves
I [2] damage to a property
J [3] feeling anxious on this day

c Listen again with the audio script on p.70 and try to guess the meaning of any words that you don't know. Then check in your dictionary.

6 READING

a Read the article once. What year do childhood memories need to survive until to stand a chance of making it into adulthood?

b Read the article again and mark the sentences **T** (true) or **F** (false).

1 At the age of five or six, children tend to still remember events that happened when they were two.

2 From the age of seven, early memories don't feature key details like location.

3 Children recalled six different life events at their later sessions with the psychologist.

4 The events discussed with the psychologist included day-to-day school life and the context of lessons.

5 By the age of eight or nine, children could only recall approximately a third of their early memories.

6 The researchers found out that the kind of details which stayed in the mind didn't alter much over the years.

c Look at the highlighted verbs and try to work out their meaning. Check in your dictionary.

When childhood memories fade

Most adults struggle to recall events from their first few years of life and now scientists have identified exactly when these childhood memories are lost forever. A new study into childhood amnesia – the phenomenon where early memories are forgotten – has found that it tends to take effect around the age of seven.

The researchers found that while most three year olds can recall a lot of what happened to them over a year earlier, these memories can persist while they are five and six, by the time they are over seven these memories decline rapidly.

The psychologists behind the research say this is because at around this age the way we form memories begins to change. Before the age of seven, children tend to have an immature form of recall where they do not have a sense of time or place in their memories. In older children, however, the early events they can recall tend to be more adult like in their content and the way they are formed. Children also have a far faster rate of forgetting than adults and so the turnover of memories tends to be higher, meaning early memories are less likely to survive.

Professor Patricia Bauer, a psychologist and associate dean for research at Emory College of Art and Science, studied 83 children over several years for the research, which was published in the scientific journal *Memory*. The youngsters first visited the laboratory at the age of three years old and discussed six unique events from their past, such as family outings, camping holidays, trips to the zoo, first day of school and birthdays. The children then returned for a second session at the ages between five years old and nine years old to discuss the same events and were asked to recall details they had previously remembered.

The researchers found that between the ages of five and seven, the amount of memories the children could recall remained between 63 and 72 per cent. However, the amount of information the children who were eight and nine years old could remember dropped dramatically to 35 and 36 per cent.

When the researchers looked closely at the kind of details the children were and were not able to remember, they found marked age differences. The memories of the younger children tended to lack autobiographical narrative such as place and time. Their memories also had less narrative, which researchers believe may lead to a process known as 'retrieval induced forgetting' – where the action of remembering causes other information to be forgotten. As the children got older, however, the memories they recalled from early childhood tended to have these features.

Professor Bauer said, 'The fact that the younger children had less complete narratives relative to the older children, likely has consequences for the continued accessibility of early memories beyond the first decade of life. We anticipate that memories that survive into the ninth or tenth year of life, when narrative skills are more developed, would continue to be accessible over time.'

The best revenge is to be
unlike him who performed the injury.
Marcus Aurelius, Roman Emperor

3A Don't get mad, get even

1 PRONUNCIATION
words and phrases of French origin

a **iChecker** Listen and write the French words.

1 /ˈkliːʃeɪ/ — *cliché*
2 /ˈrɒndeɪvuː/ — *rendez-vous*
3 /ˌfəʊ ˈpɑː/ — *f*
4 /ˌdeɪʒɑː ˈvuː/ — *deja vu*
5 /ˌɒntrəprəˈnɜː/ — *entrepreneur ?*
6 /ˈbæleɪ/ — *ballet*
7 /buˈkeɪ/ — *bouquet*
8 /fiˈɒnseɪ/ — *fiancée*
9 /kuː/ — *coup*
10 /ˌfeɪt əˈkɒmpliː/ — *fait-accompli*

b Practise saying the words in **a**.

2 VOCABULARY phrases with *get*

a Match the sentence halves.

1 I'm going to get
2 I'll call you back as soon as I get
3 I wanted to get
4 I can't get past. Can you get
5 When I went out, I got
6 The heating isn't working. Can you get
7 Max hit Stevie but Stevie got
8 My colleagues didn't trust me until they got
9 When I met up with my boss, I got

i
f
e
d
g
b
a
c
h

a his own back by kicking him.
b hold of someone in Maintenance?
c to know me better.
d out of the way, please?
e rid of my parents before my boyfriend arrived.
f the chance.
g a shock because my car wasn't on the drive.
h the impression she was angry with me.
i into trouble if I'm late again.

to get into trouble
to get rid of sb/sth
to get a shock
to get hold of smb/smth
to get one's own back by doing smb
to get to know smb better

b Complete the idioms with these words.

act	~~anywhere~~	~~house~~	~~life~~
~~message~~	~~nerves~~	~~on~~	~~way~~

to get a life
to get one' act together

1 My sister gets on my *nerves*. She's always borrowing my clothes without asking me.
2 I've bought my boyfriend an electric shaver in the hope that he'll get the *message* about his beard.
3 Laura's parents don't know how to say no. She always gets her own *way*.
4 I'm not getting *anywhere* with this essay. I don't know where to start.
5 My flatmate needs to get a *life*. He hasn't got any friends and he never goes out.
6 My dad is getting *on* a bit now. He's nearly 80.
7 Luckily, my mum and my girlfriend have got on like a *house* on fire since they first met.
8 I really need to get my *act* together if I'm going to catch the plane. I haven't packed yet!

c Complete the sentences with the missing particle.

1 At last, my sister has got *over* her ex-boyfriend and she's started going out again.
2 It's a tiny island so you can use bikes to get *around*.
3 We got *away* with not doing the homework because the teacher forgot to take it in!
4 They've got really *behind* with the project so they'll have to work late until they finish it.
5 Ryan is trying to get *out* of going on holiday with his in-laws by saying he's got too much work.
6 My gran has stopped reading all the bad news in the paper because she says it gets her *down*.
7 Stop chatting to your friends and get *on* with your homework!
8 I've tried to explain to my girlfriend how I feel but I can't get *through* to her.
9 I can't get *by* on what I earn, so I'm looking for some extra work.
10 I got *back* to my friend as soon as I read her text message.

to get the impression that...
as soon as, to get the chance - как только
будет возможность
as soon as I get the chance

17

3 LEXIS IN CONTEXT Blind Date

Look at the Lexis in Context on Student's Book p.26.
Then complete the sentences.

1 You may as well be honest instead of **dr**essing **up** the truth.

2 You can't **r**ule **o**ut the possibility that he may be seeing somebody else.

3 Pete's girlfriend has such a lovely smile that she can **w**in anybody o ver.

4 It's all very well apologizing, but who is going to *to pick up the bill* **f**oot the **b**ill for the damage?

5 I've only got ten minutes, so we'll have to make this **sh**ort and **sw**eet.

6 I'm going to the party because I don't want to **m**iss **o**ut on all the fun.

7 My husband is good at making promises, but he finds it hard to **f**ollow them **th**rough.

8 I can't **m**ake **up** my **m**ind if I want to see him again.

4 GRAMMAR get

Rewrite the **bold** phrases using the correct form of *get*.

1 We **arrived at the theatre** too late to see the show.
   got to the theatre

2 Can you **persuade Paul to look** at my computer?
   Can you get Paul to look ...

3 I'll never **become accustomed to** getting up at 5.30 in the morning. *accustomed to*
   get used to

4 The afternoon shadows **lengthened** as the sun went down.
   got longer

5 We're **having our kitchen repainted** next month.
   getting our kitchen repaired

6 I can't **make the kids eat** their dinner.
   get the kids to eat

7 I hope **I'm not sent to** Manchester – I want to stay in London.
   I haven't got to go to

8 Public transport in my town is **improving**.
   is getting better

9 **They fired my boss** for stealing money.
   got rid of my boss ...

10 Could you possibly **ask Mike to** pick me up?
   get Mike to pick me up

5 LISTENING

a **iChecker** Listen to five speakers talking about memorable dates. Which speakers had successful dates? Which dates were unsuccessful?

b Listen again and mark the sentences **T** (true) or **F** (false).

1 Speaker 1 agreed to the date straight away. F

2 Speaker 1 went out with someone who was desperately in love with her. F

3 Speaker 2 was the victim of an accident during their memorable date. T *tipped the drinks over h*

4 The incident on Speaker 2's date ruined the relationship. F

5 Speaker 3 enjoyed herself tremendously. F

6 Speaker 3 decided it was best not to meet up again. T

7 Speaker 4 organized the date spontaneously. T

8 Speaker 4 and their partner often joke about their date. T

9 Speaker 5 didn't have the same sense of humour as the person she went out with. F

10 Speaker 5 was upset not to get a marriage proposal. F

c Listen again with the audio script on p.70 and try to guess the meaning of any words that you don't know. Then check in your dictionary.

6 READING

a Read the article once. Which act of revenge caused the most damage?

b Read the article again and match the headings A–H with the stories 1–6. There are two headings you do not need to use.

A That's what friends are for
B Dedicated to the profession
C Welcome home
D Kiss and tell
E Clean plate
F Total shutdown
G Silent witnesses
H His pride and joy

c Look at the highlighted phrasal verbs and idioms. What do you think they mean? Check in your dictionary.

Revenge is sweet

According to writer Claire Gillman, getting even is becoming increasingly popular as life gets more stressful. In her book *Revenge is Sweet* Claire reveals that men are much more the vengeful sex, except over romantic matters, when it is women who are most likely to take revenge. Here are some of her favourite tales from the book.

1 W / F

The wife of a radio DJ saw red when she heard her husband flirting with a glamorous model on air. She immediately posted an advert for his £30,000 Lotus Esprit Turbo sports car on eBay for 50p and sold the car within five minutes. Later, she told journalists that she didn't care about the money. 'I just wanted to get my own back,' she admitted.

2 C

After a long-running dispute between neighbours, one of the parties went on holiday for two weeks in the summer. The other neighbour took advantage of their absence to put two pints of maggots through the neighbour's letter box. The family returned to a house full of flies.

3 D

An 80-year-old woman was in front of a judge, charged with shoplifting. He asked her what she had stolen. 'A can of peaches,' replied the woman. 'How many peaches were in the can?' asked the judge. She replied that there were six. 'Then I'll give you six days in jail,' said the judge. Before he had time to speak further, the woman's husband added, 'She also stole a tin of peas.'

4 E

Rude customers tend to drive staff in restaurants crazy. One chef confessed that after a customer had demanded that the sauce be removed from his burger, she licked the sauce off it with her tongue and then sent it back via the waiter.

5 F

A computer technician was angered when his temporary position was terminated so he deliberately brought down five of eight network servers. All the data in the servers was deleted and none was recoverable. As a result, the company was forced to shut its New York office for two days and sustained losses of more than $100,000.

6 B

A doctor was called out at 2 a.m. one night to visit a patient who lived some distance away. On his arrival, he discovered that it was, in fact, a non-urgent case, and the patient could perfectly well have waited until the next day to visit him in his surgery. Imagine the patient's surprise when the doctor popped by in the early hours of the following morning to check he was OK!

Glossary

pint a unit for measuring liquids. 1 pint = 0.568 litres
maggot a creature like a short worm which is the young form of a fly

3B History in the making

1 VOCABULARY conflict and warfare

a Complete the crossword.

Clues across ➡

Clues down ↓

b Circle the correct word.

1 During the coup, the military tried to *overthrow* / *release* the government.
2 There were very few *casualties* / *wounded* from the fighting – only two people were killed.
3 The country *declared* / *broke out* war on its neighbour because there were troops on the border.
4 The city was *blown up* / *shelled* all night.
5 The two armies agreed to a *treaty* / *ceasefire* to give them a chance to tend to the wounded.
6 The troops saw they could not win so they held up a white flag indicating that they wanted to *capture* / *surrender*.
7 The government forces *retreated* / *defeated* the rebels during the night.
8 During the siege, civilians were shot at by isolated *snipers* / *troops* hiding in the hills.
9 Soldiers *looted* / *executed* shops in their search for food.
10 The new *ally* / *commander* of the armed forces will be meeting the President later today.

2 PRONUNCIATION stress in word families

a Underline the stressed syllable in the following words.

1 ca|sual|ties
2 ci|vil
3 re|fu|gee
4 sur|vi|vor
5 com|man|der
6 cease|fire
7 vic|to|ry
8 re|lease
9 cap|ture
10 re|treat
11 ex|e|cute
12 sur|ren|der

b **iChecker** Listen and check. Practise saying the words.

c Circle the word with a different sound.

1 aɪ bike	2 uː boot	3 iː tree	4 ɔː horse
ally	troops	besiege	war
sniper	bullet	treaty	sword
shield	wounded	weapon	declare

d **iChecker** Listen and check. Practise saying the words.

3 GRAMMAR discourse markers (2): adverbs and adverbial expressions

a Complete the mini-dialogues with a discourse marker.

1 **A** Have you got your tickets for the concert yet?
   B Yes, I have. _Talking_ of the concert, have you heard their new album yet?

2 **A** How did your interview go?
   B It was brilliant. In other w_ords_, I got the job!

3 **A** Could you tell us about our board and lodging?
   B As far as meals are c_oncerned_, breakfast and dinner will be provided by the hotel.

4 **A** Are you going to Jay's party on Saturday?
   B No, I'm not. As a m_atter_ of fact, I haven't been invited.

5 **A** So, let's decide. The beach or the mountains?
   B On the wh_ole_ I'd rather go to the beach, so that we can have a swim.

6 **A** Thanks for filling me in on what I missed.
   B No problem. By the w_ay_, there's another meeting on Wednesday. Did you know?

7 **A** Can we inform our families of our destination?
   B No. This is top secret. That is to s_ay_, you are not to reveal your whereabouts to anyone.

8 **A** Did you buy anything while you were in town?
   B No, I didn't take any money with me. In any c_ase_, there wasn't anything I liked.

9 **A** How does it feel to be famous at last?
   B The attention is incredible. On the other h_and_, I miss my privacy.

10 **A** We're going to my mum's for dinner on Saturday.
   B OK. At l_east_ we won't have to cook.

b Circle the correct discourse marker.

1 _In conclusion_ / _As far as_, I think the company should invest in new machinery to update the factory.

2 _Basically_ / _At least_, Sam and Ella aren't very well-off because they're both unemployed.

3 Ask your boss if you can take the day off. _In other words_ / _I mean_, he can't say no.

4 I don't feel like cooking tonight. _On the whole_ / _Besides_, there's nothing in the fridge.

5 _Obviously_ / _Regarding_, I'm going to study Maths because there's nothing else I'm good at.

6 I've read all the applications and _by the way_ / _all in all_, I think Adam is the best person for the job.

7 You might want to dress up for dinner. _After all_ / _To sum up_, everyone will be wearing a suit.

8 _As I was saying_ / _Talking of_ before I got cut off, we need to make a decision.

9 _To sum up_ / _As regards_, we recommend accepting the pay deal in case management decide to withdraw the offer.

10 You'll need a jacket, _that is_ / _otherwise_ you might get cold.

4 LISTENING

The Last Emperor

Elizabeth

a iChecker Try to match the historical films 1–5 with the periods in which they are set a–e. Then listen to five speakers talking about the films and check your answers.

1 _Elizabeth_   b
2 _Argo_   d
3 _The Last Emperor_   a
4 _Invictus_   c
5 _Agora_   e

a early 20th century China
b 16th century England
c Roman Empire
d 1979–81 Iran hostage crisis
e late 20th century South Africa

b Listen again and match the speakers 1–5 to the reasons why these films are the speakers' favourites A–G. There are two reasons that you do not need.

Speaker 1   E
Speaker 2   C
Speaker 3   G B
Speaker 4   A
Speaker 5   F

A the acting
B the director
C the plot
D the main character
E the costumes
F the ending
G the photography

c Listen again with the audio script on p.71 and try to guess the meaning of any words that you don't know. Then check in your dictionary.

5 READING

a Match the opponents a–e to the battles 1–5, then read the article once to check your answers.

1 The Battle of Plataea — *b*
2 The Battle of Waterloo — *d*
3 The Battle of Cannae — *a*
4 The Battle of Thermopylae — *e*
5 The Battle of Gettysburg — *c*

a Carthage versus Rome
b Greece versus Persia
c The Union versus the Confederacy ✓
d France versus Britain and Prussia ✓
e Sparta versus Persia

b Read the article again and choose the correct answer from the battles A–E. The battles may be chosen more than once.

In which battle…?

1 did reinforcements arrive once the battle had started *B*
2 was one of the armies tiny *D*
3 was one of the armies more confident than the other *A* (*higher morale*)
4 did both sides lose almost the same number of soldiers *E*
5 did the army catch their enemy by surprise *E C*
6 did the losing army contain three times as many soldiers as the victors *A*
7 was one side defeated through treachery *D*
8 had one army previously had to make a perilous journey *C*
9 did the commanders' mistakes contribute to their defeat *B*
10 did a group of soldiers attack a certain part of the other army *E*

c Look at the highlighted words and phrases and match them to the definitions below.

1 bad luck *noun* *ill fate*
2 rushed forward and attacked *verb* *to charge*
3 strongly influencing the way something develops *verb* *to mould the future*
4 killed a large number of people violently *verb* *slaughter*
5 showing no kindness or pity *adverb* *mercilessly*
6 the amount of confidence and enthusiasm a person has at a particular time *noun* *morale*
7 a narrow passage through mountains *noun* *narrow pass / backdoor entrance*
8 of great importance because other things depend on it *adjective* *pivotal battle / pivotal*

Five important battles from history

Every age of human history has experienced battles that have been instrumental in moulding the future. Below are five of the bloodiest and most pivotal battles ever fought.

A The Battle of Plataea (479 BCE)
This battle occurred during the Greco-Persian Wars. An army of 40,000 Greek soldiers, of which 10,000 were Spartans, faced the invading force of Persia with 120,000 men. Although outnumbered, the Spartans and Athenians were more tactical, heavily armed and had higher morale. The Persian army had just suffered a previous defeat and some inner conflicts and divisions. The Greeks slaughtered the Persians at Plataea and succeeded in driving them out of Greece.

B The Battle of Waterloo (18 June 1815)
This battle was fought between the French army, led by Napoleon Bonaparte, and the British and Prussian forces led by Wellington and von Blucher respectively. Napoleon took the initiative during the early part of the battle, but things began to go awry later in the day when the army suffered the effects of bad weather, blunders by some of the generals, ill fate, and the timely arrival of the Prussian forces (50,000 men). After suffering heavy casualties, Napoleon was forced to leave Waterloo and surrender.

C The Battle of Cannae (2 August 216 BCE)
This battle is regarded as one of the greatest tactical military achievements in war history. The Carthaginian commander Hannibal Barca led a massive troop of soldiers, accompanied by hundreds, or possibly thousands, of war elephants, across the mountainous Alps. He took a backdoor entrance into northern Italy and slaughtered the Romans at Cannae, killing 70,000 of the 87,000 soldiers in the Roman army.

D The Battle of Thermopylae (480 BCE)
This battle occurred on the eve of the Greco-Persian wars when King Leonidas of Sparta faced the invading Persian troops with only 300 Spartan soldiers. The King and his men blocked the only narrow pass through which the Persians could go, killing a total of 20,000 Persians. The Spartans only lost when one of their soldiers betrayed them by showing the Persians a secret passage. Leonidas and his men were all mercilessly slaughtered.

E The Battle of Gettysburg (July 1863)
This battle was fought during the American Civil War between the Confederate troops from the South, led by General Robert Lee, and the Union troops, led by General George Meade. One of the most dramatic moments was the Pickett's Charge, when 12,500 Confederate infantry charged towards the Union's centre formation. In the end, the Union side won, but lost a total of 23,055 soldiers. The defeated Confederate army lost 23,231 soldiers.

1 LOOKING AT LANGUAGE
collocations

Complete the collocations in the sentences.

1 The problems we **f**ace today are quite different from those that troubled our ancestors.
2 We have an **a** w*ful* lot of revision to do for our History exam.
3 The leader of the opposition seems to be **d**eadly serious about resigning if his party doesn't win the next election.
4 We could talk for hours about the **r**ights and wrongs of the political system in ancient Rome.
5 Politicians need to concentrate on the big **p**icture and not get distracted by small details.
6 Manchester Town Hall is a **cl**iché example of Gothic revival architecture.
7 Freedom of speech and the right to vote are two important **c**ivil rights.
8 In medieval times, life was good for the landowners, but **o**rdinary people had a difficult time.

2 READING

a Read the article. Mark the sentences **T** (true) or **F** (false).

1 The author of *Horrible Histories* used to work on the stage.   T
2 Deary's *Horrible Histories* books are purely fictional.   F
   had just written
3 Deary began writing the stories in the same year as his country celebrated an important occasion.   F
4 Teachers bought *Blitzed Brits* to teach their classes about World War II.   T
5 The host of the TV shows is a famous figure from history.   *(a rat).*   F
6 In many of the comedy sketches, a parallel is drawn between past and present events.   T
7 The author did not expect his concept to be so popular.   T
8 Plans to build a *Horrible Histories* theme park have been announced.   *rumours*   F

b Underline five words or phrases you don't know. Use your dictionary to look up their meaning and pronunciation.

Why Horrible Histories is a hit

Getting an audience interested in history can be a daunting task at the best of times, but it's especially difficult when your medium is the written word. Enter Terry Deary, former actor and full-time author of the best-selling series *Horrible Histories*. Since the publication of *Terrible Tudors* and *Awesome Egyptians* in 1993, readers have been hooked on the series, which now consists of over 60 titles. More than 20 million copies have been sold in around 30 different languages. So just what is the secret behind Deary's success?

The answer lies in the way the subject is presented. For each of his tales, Deary selects an important era from the past and picks out the most unpleasant events: gory killings, juicy scandal and grim tales of revenge. These lesser-known aspects of history are recounted in comic-book fashion, eliciting disbelief in the reader, although the details are completely accurate. And this is what appeals to children about his books: the fact that by reading them, they learn something unbelievable but true.

As well as Deary's writing style, it was also coincidence that contributed to his rise to fame. Two years after the series began, the 50th anniversary of the end of World War II came along. Deary had conveniently just written *Blitzed Brits*, a description of events in wartime Britain. Teachers were looking for something on the subject to grab their students' attention in class and *Blitzed Brits* fitted the bill perfectly. The book shot up the sales charts and made Deary into a bestselling author almost overnight.   *1995   Blitzed Brits*

Yet *Horrible Histories* is not confined to books. Deary's gruesome tales have also been adapted for television, providing the material for five whole series. The shows are presented by a talking rat called Rattus Rattus, whose job is to introduce comedy sketches portraying a particular historical event and to verify the facts they contain. The sketches often parody current media stories, and each episode contains a song that imitates a particular pop style, which can be anything from boy bands to hard rock. The outrageous costumes and ridiculous humour of the show appeal to both children and grown-ups alike, and the TV series has won numerous awards at both children's and adult ceremonies.   *to parody*

Not even Terry Deary anticipated the huge success of *Horrible Histories*, which has joined the ranks of other children's favourites such as *Harry Potter* and *The Hunger Games*. Along with reading the books and following the TV series, fans can also purchase magazines, listen along to audio books, play video games and watch stage productions. There have even been rumours of a theme park. With a range of products that wide, who would dare claim that history is boring?

No man should live where he can hear
his neighbor's dog bark.

Nathaniel Macon, American politician

4A Sounds interesting

1 VOCABULARY sounds and the human voice

a (Circle) the correct word.

1 The children ran out of the room because of the large bee *hissing |* (*buzzing*) around the window.

2 She was *banging |* (*tapping*) her finger on the table, waiting for her brother to answer his phone.

3 There was a loud (*bang*) *| slam* as the fireworks went off.

4 I can't stand people who (*slurp*) *| drip* their soup when they eat it.

5 I had to get up and lock the door because it was *hooting |* (*rattling*) in the wind.

6 The cat arched its back and (*hissed*) *| whistled* at us as we walked in.

7 The engine *crashed |* (*roared*) into life when he switched it on.

8 Johnny's got a cold, so he's been *snoring |* (*sniffing*) all day.

9 The little girl liked the way the sweets *splashed |* (*crunched*) in her mouth.

10 It was so quiet in the room that you could hear the (*ticking*) *| clicking* of the clock.

11 We heard the (*screeching*) *| creaking* of tyres as Janet's boyfriend drew up outside her front door.

12 After the argument, Carl stormed out of the room and (*slammed*) *| hummed* the door.

b Complete the sentences with the verbs in the list.

~~giggled~~	~~groaned~~	~~mumbled~~	~~screamed~~	sighed
~~sobbed~~	~~stammered~~	~~whispered~~	~~yelled~~	

1 'STOP MAKING SO MUCH NOISE!' the old man *yelled* from an upstairs window.

2 'What have you done *this* time?' *sighed* Stephen's mother with resignation.

3 'My new doll is broken,' *sobbed* the little girl, tears rolling down her cheeks.

4 'My ankle hurts,' the player *groaned* as he lay on the ground.

5 'There's a spider in the bath!' my sister *screamed* in horror.

6 'I didn't have t-t-time to do my h-h-homework,' Phil *stammered* nervously.

7 Half way through the exam, David *whispered* to Alison, 'What's the answer to number 5?'

8 'Look at her hat!' the students *giggled* . 'It looks really funny.'

9 'Sorry,' he *mumbled* , but nobody could understand what he said.

2 PRONUNCIATION
consonant clusters

a **iChecker** Listen and write the missing words with consonant clusters.

1 Some of the pictures on *display* have been lent by other galleries. *strech*

2 It's always a good idea to *check* before and after doing exercise.

3 'What a wonderful surprise,' she *exclaimed*.

4 My son's just failed his driving test for the *sixth* time!

5 We're going to IKEA to get some new *shelves* for my study.

6 The best speech was the one given by the *bridegroom*.

7 We *spread* out the map on the dining room table, and planned our route.

8 The man *punched* the burglar on the nose.

b Practise saying the sentences in **a**.

3 LEXIS IN CONTEXT
I have a phobia of sound

Look at the Lexis in Context on Student's Book p.34. Then complete the words.

1 The passengers wanted to know why the train had stopped so a*bruptly* .

2 It can be very tiring being with my brothers because they are c*onstently* arguing. *continually*

3 He had been revising for months, so he passed his exams w *with* e*ase* .

4 St*rangely* , I actually like commuting: it gives me some valuable time to myself.

5 The area has a number of Italian restaurants i*n* close pr*oximity* to each other.

6 Her s*eemingly* stupid question produced an extremely useful answer.

7 I try to avoid giving my neighbour a lift because she chatters i*ncessantly* the whole journey.

4 GRAMMAR speculation and deduction

a Complete the mini-dialogues using *must | might | could | may | can't* or *should* and the correct form of the verbs in brackets.

1 A Jessica's looking pleased with herself.
B Yes. She _must have done_ well in her job interview. (do)

2 A Where's Eve? She said to meet her just outside the tube station.
B I suppose she ~~could/might~~ _may be waiting_ at a different entrance. (wait)

3 A Harry left work about an hour ago.
B Yes, he _should ~~be~~ have been_ here by now. It only takes 20 minutes. (be)

4 A How about this dress for your cousin?
B I don't know. I've never seen her in a dress. She _might/may not like_ it. (not like)

5 A My brother's in his room doing his homework.
B Well, he _can't be studying_. I can hear him talking on the phone! (study)

6 A Jason isn't answering his phone.
B Well, he's gone swimming and _might/may not have taken_ it with him to the pool. (not take)

7 A My secretary is off sick.
B Well, she _can't have_ anything serious. I've just seen her playing tennis. (have)

8 A Tony didn't show up at the party. He _must have forgotten_ about it. (forget) *might/could*
B Yes, he's very absent-minded.

b Complete the second sentence using the **bold** word so that it means the same as the first.

1 I don't think Luke will pass his driving test. **probably**
Luke _probably won't pass his driving test._

2 I'm sure we'll win the match. **bound**
We _are bound to win the match_

3 I'm sure you'll enjoy the film. **definitely**
You _will definitely enjoy the film_

4 I don't think it'll rain tonight. **likely** → unlikely
It _is not likely to rain tonight._

5 They probably won't agree to our proposal. **unlikely**
They _are unlikely to agree to our proposal_

6 My father is likely to take early retirement. **probably**
My father _will probably take early retirement_

7 Your parents will almost certainly complain about it. **sure**
Your parents _are sure to complain about it_

8 The manager is sure not to give us a pay rise. **definitely**
The manager _won't definitely give us a pay rise,_

5 LISTENING

repercussion – ответная реакция, последствие
percussion instrument – ударные инструменты

a **iChecker** Listen to someone talking about the percussionist Evelyn Glennie. In what way is she an unusual musician?

b Listen again and complete the summary.

Dame Evelyn Glennie was born in Aberdeen, Scotland. She studied at the Royal Academy of Music. She has been performing for more than [1] _20_ years, and plays over [2] _60_ different percussion instruments. She not only plays and records classical and pop music, but has also composed several film [3] _soundtracks_. Dame Evelyn finds it frustrating that journalists often write about her [4] _deafness_ more than her music. She thinks that there is no real difference between hearing and [5] _feeling_ a vibration. Dame Evelyn never wears [6] _shoes_ when she performs, in order to feel the vibrations of her instruments. *bare foot*

c Listen again with the audio script on p.71 and try to guess the meaning of any words that you don't know. Then check in your dictionary.

6 READING

a Read the article once. What is piped music? According to the writer, in which place might piped music have the most serious consequences? *in surgeries*

Silence is golden

You hear it everywhere: in pubs, restaurants and hotels, in the plane, on the train, or on the bus. It comes at you unexpectedly down the phone, and it's even on television ruining perfectly decent programmes. This unsolicited noise is, of course, piped music, an incessant jingle that is almost impossible to escape.

Contrary to popular belief, it appears that more people dislike this kind of music than actually appreciate it. In a poll carried out by a British newspaper, piped music came third in the list of things people most detested about modern life. (The first two most hated things were other forms of noise.) What is more, a recent survey into shopping habits shows that at least 50 per cent of customers would walk out of a store that had piped music. With figures like these, there can be no doubt about the widespread aversion to the noise.

It is people with some kind of hearing impairment who suffer most from the din. This group includes the elderly, who often develop an age-related hearing problem called presbycusis. The condition prevents them distinguishing the individual words of a conversation above the noise of any background music. As time goes by, they find it more and more difficult to interact. In fact, a 2013 survey commissioned by a British bank showed that around 61 per cent of older people consider piped music in shops and banks their biggest bugbear. The reason most of them gave was that it makes them feel alienated.

However, piped music may also be responsible for far more serious health problems. It has long been recognized that unwanted noise produces stress. The listener experiences a rise in blood pressure and a depression of the immune system. A survey of 215 blood donors at Nottingham University Medical School found that playing piped music made donors more nervous before giving blood. They also felt more depressed afterwards. These results suggest that a hospital might not be the right place to play this kind of sound.

Yet a care institution in London has recently announced that it is going to do just that. The hospital plans to introduce piped music into its Accident and Emergency Department to 'calm distressed patients'. The music will be provided by legendary musician Brian Eno, who has been supplying 'ambient music' to airports for nearly four decades. The hospital's objective is to make A & E more patient-friendly, but it is likely to have quite the opposite effect.

Fortunately, help is at hand in the form of Pipedown, a campaign for freedom from piped music. The movement is pushing for legislation to ban its use in public places, especially in hospitals and doctors' surgeries where patients are in no position to argue or go somewhere else. If the campaign is successful, the London hospital will have to drop its plans. But for many, this will not be a bad thing.

b Read the article again and mark the sentences **T** (true) or **F** (false).

1 According to the writer, the main problem with piped music is you can't get away from it. *T*
2 The results of the newspaper poll show that the top three annoyances are all noise-related. *T*
3 Piped music encourages the majority of people to shop in a store. *F*
4 Elderly people tend to dislike piped music because it's not their kind of music. *T*
5 Piped music can help blood donors to relax. *F*
6 The writer thinks Brian Eno's music probably won't improve the atmosphere of A & E. *T*
7 The main aim of the Pipedown campaign is to get rid of piped music in all public places. *T*

c Find words or phrases in the article which mean:

1 piped music
ambient music ___ music
background ___ music
2 a recognizable tune that is easy to remember
bugbear
3 a loud and unpleasant noise
incessant jingle

4B From cover to cover?

1 VOCABULARY
describing books and films

Complete the sentences.

1 The story was really h*aunting*. I can't stop thinking about it.
2 The book was extremely th*ought* -pr*ovoking* and it made me think seriously about human rights issues.
3 This is the perfect holiday read – a really e*ntertaining* book.
4 The ending was completely i*ntriguing*. That would never have happened in real life and it ruined the whole film for me.
5 The plot is i*ntriguing* I never know what's going to happen next.
6 The book's focus on the cruel and violent events that occur in a war make for a really d*epressing* read.
7 The plot was absolutely gr*ipping*. I couldn't put the book down.
8 The writer's style is difficult to read. I find his books very h*eavy*-g*oing*.
9 The final scene was incredibly m*oving* – I cried all the way out of the cinema!
10 His new novel is very f*ast*-m*oving* – so much happens in each short chapter.

2 PRONUNCIATION /ɔː/

a Write the words with the /ɔː/ sound.

1 /'drɔːbæk/   *drawback*
2 /wɔːk/   *walk*
3 /ɪmˈplɔːzəbl/   *implausible*
4 /rɪˈzɔːsfl/   *resourceful*
5 /rɪˈwɔːdɪŋ/   *rewarding*
6 /ˈdɔːtə/   *daughter*
7 /ˈθɔːt-prəvəʊkɪŋ/   *thought-provoking*
8 /ˈwɜːkfɔːs/   *workforce*

b **iChecker** Listen and check. Practise saying the words.

c **iChecker** Listen and write five sentences.

1 _____
2 _____
3 _____
4 _____
5 _____

d Practise saying the sentences in **c**.

3 GRAMMAR adding emphasis (1): inversion

a Complete the sentences with the adverbial expressions in the list. In some sentences more than one answer may be possible.

| Hardly | Never | No sooner | Not only |
| Not until | Only | Rarely | Scarcely |

1 *Hardly* had we set off when the engine started rattling.
2 *Not until* the clock struck midnight did the musicians start playing.
3 *Never* have I heard such a moving speech. The last time was at the funeral of a close relation.
4 *No sooner* had we sat down to eat than the doorbell rang.
5 *Only* when you get on the scales do you realize how much weight you've put on over Christmas.
6 *Scarcely* had she entered the classroom when the students started to pester her.
7 *Not only* was my father in pain, but his pride had also been hurt.
8 *Rarely* had the fans witnessed such a resounding victory in the history of the club.

27

b Rewrite the sentences to make them more emphatic.

1 The exam began when all the papers had been given out.
   Only _when all the papers had been given out did the_
   exam begin .

2 He betrayed my trust and he wrecked my car.
   Not only _did he betray my trust but_
   he also wrecked my car .

3 The sun had only just gone down when the temperature fell dramatically.
   Scarcely _had the sun gone done when_
   the temprature fell dramatically .

4 I have never seen such a wonderful sight.
   Never _have I seen such a wonderful sight_
   .

5 As soon as the teacher turned her back, the children started whispering.
   No sooner _had the teacher turned her back,_
   than the children started whispering .

6 The woman had just sat down when her baby started crying.
   Hardly _had the woman sat down when her_
   baby started crying .

7 You rarely find two people so alike.
   Rarely _do you find 2 people so alike_ .

8 Classes will not recommence until a replacement teacher has been found.
   Not until _a replacement teacher has been_
   found will classes recommence .

4 LEXIS IN CONTEXT Translation Diary

Look at the Lexis in Context on Student's Book p.41.
Then complete the words.

1 The man turned around and **l**eft when nobody answered the door.
2 All of the rooms in the hotel were **i**_____.
3 He **i**mplored the kidnapper not to hurt him.
4 The child sat **m**ute in the corner of the room.
5 His illness has left him completely **i**mmobile, and he has to remain in bed.
6 Can I borrow that book when you're **d**one **w**ith it?
7 She said nothing and **m**erely smiled in response to his question.
8 I tried to give the police an **a**ccurate description of the attacker.
9 Beware! Thieves may try to steal your **b**ackpack without you noticing.
10 That shop sells bags of every **c**onceivable shape and size.

5 LISTENING

a iChecker Listen to a radio programme about film adaptations of books. According to Lindsey, are these book-to-film adaptations successful or not?

1 *The Lord of the Rings* _____
2 *The Hunger Games* _____

b Listen again and mark the sentences **T** (true) or **F** (false).

1 According to Lindsey, a good film adaptation is exactly the same as the book. F
2 A good adaptation has to get the timing right. T
3 Choosing the right cast can make a big difference to the success of a film adaptation. T
4 The main reason for the success of *The Lord of the Rings* series is its setting. F
5 Special effects were used extensively in the creation of the character Gollum. T
6 The main reason why Lindsey doesn't like *The Hunger Games* films is the casting. F

c Listen again with the audio script on p.71 and try to guess the meaning of any words that you don't know. Then check in your dictionary.

6 READING

a Read the text once. What advice does the writer give?

b Read the text again and choose the best answer.

1 As an adult, the writer regards her childhood ideas about reading as… .
   a extremely resourceful
   b quite thorough
   c rather immature
   d very sophisticated

2 The writer hates Russell Banks' *Book of Jamaica* because… .
   a she didn't understand the plot
   b she made herself finish it
   c she doesn't think much of the author
   d she had an awful summer job at the time

3 The writer's advice to readers who aren't enjoying a particular book is to… .
   a find an alternative
   b take a break
   c try a different book by the same author
   d finish it at all costs

4 According to the writer, the first 50 pages of a book is… .
   a the minimum that her friends suggest reading
   b enough to find out what a book is about
   c what she advises people to read to find out if they will like a book
   d the minimum she needs to read to know if she's going to like a book

5 The writer considers that people may end up reading less if… . *at all*
   a they watch a lot of TV adaptations
   b they think reading is a waste of time
   c they persevere with books they aren't enjoying
   d they are given too many bad books to read

c Look at the highlighted idioms and phrasal verbs in the text. What do you think they mean? Check in your dictionary, then use them to complete the sentences.

1 If the title doesn't ___*grab you*___, the story surely will.
2 Whenever I ___*take a shine to*___ an author, I go on to read all of their books.
3 Have you ever read a review that ___*put you off*___ reading a novel?
4 If you've read it, ___*for pity's sake*___ don't tell me what happens in the end!
5 I watched the film ___*to its bitter end*___ although I can't say that I really enjoyed it.
6 All our proposals were dismissed ___*out of hand*___.

Lionel Shriver
On how not to read

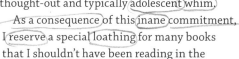

The most stupid childhood vow I ever made was to finish every book I started. Maintained well into adulthood, this policy turned reading the first page of any volume into a miniature death sentence. I imagined my compulsive completion to be a sign of adult seriousness. In truth, it was a vanity – a poorly thought-out and typically adolescent whim.

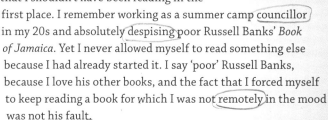

As a consequence of this inane commitment, I reserve a special loathing for many books that I shouldn't have been reading in the first place. I remember working as a summer camp councillor in my 20s and absolutely despising poor Russell Banks' *Book of Jamaica*. Yet I never allowed myself to read something else because I had already started it. I say 'poor' Russell Banks, because I love his other books, and the fact that I forced myself to keep reading a book for which I was not remotely in the mood was not his fault.

I have occasionally heard from a reader who is furious because he or she did not enjoy one of my novels yet still read to its bitter end. I reject this fury out of hand. For pity's sake, if you don't take a shine to a novel, there are loads more in the world; read something else. Continue suffering and it's not the author's fault. It's yours.

Granted, it's a good idea to give some books a chance even if they don't grab you at first, especially if they come recommended by someone you trust. But 50 pages is plenty. With some books I have an allergic reaction after two or three.

Reading time is precious. Don't waste it. Reading bad books, or books that are wrong for a certain time in your life, can dangerously put you off the activity altogether. The sign that I don't like the book I'm reading is finding myself watching reruns of *Come Dine With Me*.

> **Glossary**
>
> ***Come Dine With Me*** a popular British reality TV show that has been running since 2005.

The bad news is time flies.
The good news is you're the pilot.
Michael Altshuler, American entrepreneur

5A One thing at a time

1 LEXIS IN CONTEXT
Multitasking and mindfulness

Look at the Lexis in Context on Student's Book p.44. Then complete the sentences with the prepositions.

1 Please stop interrupting me; I can't concentrate
   _on_ my work.
2 Owing to poor sales during the recession, the company was faced _____ closure.
3 My grandfather is in a home because he is no longer capable _____ looking after himself.
4 While he was walking home, he became aware _____ a figure behind him.
5 She works on the front desk, dealing _____ customer enquiries.
6 The documentary focuses _____ the rise in knife crime in the UK.

2 GRAMMAR distancing

a Complete the sentences with the words in the list.

according	agreed	apparently	appears
believed	expected	may	seem

1 There are _believed_ to be many homeless people living on the streets of the capital.
2 It _____ that there is a connection between eating too many carbohydrates and depression.
3 The Prime Minister is _____ to announce his resignation by the end of the day.
4 _____ to local residents, the man had always been a little strange.
5 The thieves _____ have been disturbed while they were going through the rooms upstairs.
6 It would _____ that there is some confusion about our new dress code. Staff are still turning up in jeans.
7 It is _____ that climate change is one of the greatest dangers facing the planet.
8 _____, the footballer was arrested because of an incident at a party last night.

b Complete the second sentence so that you distance yourself from the information. Use the correct form of the verb in brackets.

1 An employee leaked the information to the press. (say)
   It is said that an employee leaked the information to the press.
2 Politicians have been falsifying their expenses. (appear)
   _____ politicians have been falsifying their expenses.
3 The country's largest bank has gone bankrupt. (announce)
   _____ the country's largest bank has gone bankrupt.
4 The pop star has had another breakdown. (think)
   The pop star _____ had another breakdown.
5 The accused was under the influence of drugs. (may)
   The accused _____ under the influence of drugs.
6 The winner had been chosen before voting commenced. (seem)
   _____ the winner had been chosen before voting commenced.
7 The burglars entered through an open window. (might)
   The burglars _____ through an open window.
8 The economic situation will improve by next year. (hope)
   _____ the economic situation will improve by next year.

3 VOCABULARY expressions with *time*

a Complete the sentences with the correct form of the verbs in the list.

give	have	make	run	save	spare	take	waste

1 I spent all morning cleaning the windows and now it's raining. I shouldn't have _wasted_ my time.
2 We _____ a lot of time by getting the direct train to King's Cross instead of changing at Birmingham.
3 Alex has basketball training every day and also at weekends. The sport _____ up all his time.
4 Kate has too much to do. She can't even _____ the time to Skype her friends.
5 My dad had never been to his club's stadium, but now he's bought a season ticket, to _____ up for lost time.

6 Mum _____ me a really hard time for failing my exams.

7 Jenna's enjoying herself a lot at university. She's _____ the time of her life.

8 I only managed to answer half the exam questions before I _____ out of time.

b Complete the sentences with a suitable preposition.

1 My manager's been really stressed recently, so she's having some time _off_ .

2 My parents like to go abroad occasionally. _____ time _____ time they visit their friends in Greece.

3 I couldn't answer my phone when you rang. I was in a meeting _____ the time.

4 Karen is very punctual. She's always _____ time.

5 _____ five days' time I'll be on a plane to Hawaii for my holiday.

6 There was a huge traffic jam and _____ the time we arrived home it was dark.

7 You weren't even born when The Police were big. They were way _____ your time.

8 She can be a bit annoying _____ times, but I still love my sister.

c Complete the time expressions in the mini-dialogues.

1 **A** Where are you going?
  B Shopping! I need some _me_ time.

2 **A** Can you come to my presentation later?
  B Sorry, I can't. I'm a bit _____ of time today.

3 **A** Was the bride late for the wedding?
  B No, she got to the church with time to _____.

4 **A** Why are you so bored these days?
  B I've got too much time on my _____ now I'm retired.

5 **A** Are you going to look for a new job?
  B No, I'm staying where I am for the time _____.

6 **A** Do you think the business is in trouble?
  B Yes, I do. It's just a _____ of time before it closes.

7 **A** Why can't I stay any longer?
  B Time's _____. Visitors have to leave at 8 p.m.

8 **A** Why aren't you going to see Andy again?
  B Because he spends the _____ time talking about himself!

4 PRONUNCIATION
linking in short phrases

a Draw a line between the words that are linked.

1 Oliver's‿asking for some‿extra time‿off.

2 My cousin Nick is never on time.

3 I find doing housework takes up a lot of time.

4 We walked to town as we had plenty of time.

5 We seem to have run out of time.

6 It's a question of time before the sports centre opens.

b **iChecker** Listen and check. Practise saying the sentences.

c **iChecker** Listen and write six sentences.

1 _____
2 _____
3 _____
4 _____
5 _____
6 _____

d Listen again and repeat the sentences in **c**.

5 LISTENING

a **iChecker** Listen to a radio programme about some new research into time. What is the science expert's 'good news'?

b Listen again and complete the summary.

How we perceive time

The brain takes time to process information from the [1]_____. The [2]_____ it takes to process the information, the slower time seems to pass.

How our perception changes with age

Children receive a lot of [3]_____ information which takes a long time to process. For them, time passes [4]_____.

Adults receive information which is more [5]_____, so it doesn't take long to process. For them, time passes more [6]_____.

What can we do to slow down time?

Keep [7]_____.
Visit [8]_____.
Meet [9]_____.
Be [10]_____.

c Listen again with the audio script on p.72 and try to guess the meaning of any words that you don't know. Then check in your dictionary.

6 READING

a Read the article once. How does the author answer the question in the title?

b Read the article again and choose the right answers.

1 How did the writer and the other participants of the meetings react to their colleague's lateness?
   a They spoke to the person about it.
   b They complained to their superiors.
   c They accepted it.
   d They weren't affected by it.

2 According to Irvin Yalom, what is responsible for the way we behave?
   a Our body clock.
   b The way our minds work.
   c Our religious convictions.
   d The pressures of time.

3 What does the writer imply was the reason that Berlusconi made Merkel wait?
   a He received an important phone call.
   b He wasn't ready for their meeting.
   c He wanted to show his importance.
   d He was having his photo taken.

4 How do most people react when their lateness is out of their control?
   a They don't really mind.
   b They get very nervous.
   c They blame someone else.
   d They have different reactions.

5 How does lateness have a 'social value'?
   a It affects other people.
   b It makes us look good.
   c It influences how we feel.
   d It isn't important to us.

c Choose the right answers.

What do you think the writer means by…?

1 The whole day lost its shape. (para 1)
   a The day's schedule was ruined.
   b The day was a complete disaster.
   c The day became shorter.

2 …are acting out an inner agenda (para 2)
   a are pretending to be something they're not
   b are trying to hide something
   c are controlling a situation for their own benefit

3 It speaks volumes. (para 2)
   a His phone call was very loud.
   b His behaviour tells you a lot.
   c His phone call goes on for a long time.

4 …the power of their absence. (para 3)
   a the effect they have on the people they're with
   b the effect they have on the people who are waiting for them
   c the effect they have on their own lives

Is being late fashionable or rude?

Being repeatedly late may just be accidental – or it could show a deep-seated psychological desire to express your own superiority

[1] When I worked in an office, meetings would often start late, usually because of a certain individual. Then they would overrun and the whole day lost its shape. But the individual was high-ranking and self-important: nobody challenged. So what are the ethics of lateness?

[2] There's a psychotherapist called Irvin Yalom who argues that all behaviour reflects psychology. Just as people who like to be on time are motivated by certain deep-seated beliefs, so those who make others wait are acting out an inner agenda, often based on an acute sense of power. There's famous footage in which Silvio Berlusconi keeps Angela Merkel waiting while he makes a call on his mobile. It speaks volumes.

[3] But that suggests all lateness is in one's control. What about when your train is cancelled or your flight is delayed or you had to wait longer for the plumber to arrive? In such cases, there's not a lot of psychology involved. Or is there? Some people will genuinely worry about the impact it will have on those left waiting, while others might secretly enjoy the power of their absence.

[4] The essential fact is that lateness means breaking a convention – you can only be late in respect of a time agreed with other people. Regardless of psychology, it has a social value. And when we treat other people's time as less valuable than our own, we treat them as inferior.

d Without looking back at the text, can you remember the nouns from the following verbs and adjectives?

1 superior _____
2 behave _____
3 late _____
4 believe _____
5 absent _____

No woman marries for money; they are all clever enough, before marrying a millionaire, to fall in love with him first.

Cesare Pavese, Italian writer

5B A material world

1 LEXIS IN CONTEXT

Do women really want to marry for money?

Look at the Lexis in Context on Student's Book p.49. Then complete the words.

1 You've got a very **s**<u>our</u> face – what's the matter?
2 Problems occur when important meetings and children's birthdays **c**_____.
3 Who **sh**_____ the responsibility of bringing up the kids in your relationship?
4 The park was **l**_____ **w**_____ plastic cups after the concert.
5 Working mothers have to **j**_____ their jobs with the needs of their children.
6 She's a successful businesswoman with a **h**_____-**fl**_____ career.

2 GRAMMAR unreal uses of past tenses

a Complete the mini-dialogues with the correct form of the words in brackets.

1 **A** Your parents will be here in an hour.
  B I know. _It's time I tidied up._ (time / I / tidy up)
2 **A** I'll call you in the morning.
  B _____ in person.
  (I / rather / you / come round)
3 **A** Our new dishwasher doesn't work very well.
  B I know. _____ it.
  (I / wish / we / not buy)
4 **A** It's a shame we can't meet up more often.
  B Yes. _____ nearer each other.
  (only / we / live)
5 **A** I won't tell your girlfriend you were here.
  B Thank you. _____
  (I / rather / she / not know)
6 **A** Did you get the grades to go to university?
  B No. _____ harder for my exams.
  (only / I / work)
7 **A** I'm fed up with working all the time.
  B _____ a holiday.
  (time / you / have)
8 **A** We can't afford a holiday this year.
  B I know. _____ better off.
  (I / wish / we / be)

b Complete the second sentence so it means the same as the first, using the words in brackets.

1 I should have applied for a grant. (wish)
  I wish I had applied _____ for a grant.
2 We are unhappy because we owe the bank a lot of money. (if only)
  _____ the bank so much money.
3 Sally ought to make up her mind about her job. (time)
  _____ her mind about her job.
4 Would you prefer us to take you home now or later? (rather)
  _____ you home now or later?
5 We regret spending all our savings on our honeymoon. (if only)
  _____ all our savings on our honeymoon.
6 Don't you think you ought to apologize to Anna? (time)
  Isn't _____ to Anna?
7 I would like to be able to see my family more. (wish)
  _____ my family more.
8 We'd prefer you not to bring your dog in here. (rather)
  _____ bring your dog in here.

3 VOCABULARY money

a Complete the missing words.

1 Would you like to pay monthly or in an annual l<u>ump</u> s<u>um</u> ?

2 My uncle works in the **st**_____ **m**_____ , buying and selling shares all day.

3 You can get a better **e**_____ **r**_____ at some Bureaux de Change than at others.

4 If you are **i**_____ **d**_____ , you owe someone money.

5 Despite the recession, many people's **st**_____ of **l**_____ has remained high.

6 Many people are struggling because wages aren't rising at the same rate as **i**_____ .

7 We live in a **c**_____ **s**_____ where people are obsessed with money.

8 **I**_____ **r**_____ have been cut to try and encourage people to borrow more money.

9 My sister has managed to get a government **g**_____ to study abroad for a year.

10 I give a **d**_____ to my favourite animal charity every year.

b Order the letters to make synonyms of *rich* or *poor*. Write **R** (rich) or **P** (poor) after each one.

1 F L T U F E N A   *affluent*   R

2 E S N I L E P N S   _____   ____

3 A D E O D L   _____   ____

4 A D R H P U   _____   ____

5 L W E Y T A H   _____   ____

6 L E W L - F O F   _____   ____

7 R E B O K   _____   ____

c Complete the second sentence so that it means the same as the first. Use an idiom with the **bold** words.

1 Our friends buy many things they can't afford. **means**
Our friends are *living beyond their means* .

2 We're overdrawn. **red**
We're _____ .

3 Don't spend all your money. It's hard work to make more. **grow**
Don't spend all your money. It _____ .

4 That yacht must have been really expensive. **arm**
That yacht must have _____ .

5 We'll never be able to buy a house unless we start saving. **belts**
We'll never be able to buy a house unless _____ .

6 Bill never eats out. He thinks it's too expensive. **robbery**
Bill never eats out. He thinks it's _____ .

7 My in-laws are extremely mean. **fist**
My in-laws are very _____ .

8 We hardly earn enough to buy what we need. **ends**
We're struggling to _____ .

4 PRONUNCIATION
US and UK accents

iChecker Can you tell the difference between US and UK accents? Listen and write **US** (US accent) or **UK** (UK accent).

1 _US_   6 _____
2 _____   7 _____
3 _____   8 _____
4 _____   9 _____
5 _____   10 _____

5 LISTENING

a **iChecker** Listen to a radio phone-in programme about saving money. Answer the questions with the names in the list.

| Emily | Jonathan | Mary | Philip | Wendy |

Which caller has a tip for saving money…?

1 at meal times
2 at the supermarket
3 for holidays
4 at home
5 on all kinds of purchases

b Listen again and answer the questions.

According to the callers, …?

1 at what temperature should your thermostat be set
2 what should you take to work to eat
3 where should you put your small change
4 how should you pay for everything you buy
5 when shouldn't you do your food shopping

c Listen again with the audio script on p.72 and try to guess the meaning of any words that you don't know. Then check in your dictionary.

6 READING

a Read the article once. Choose the sentence which best summarizes the results of the research.

   A If everyone in the country has more money as a result of economic development, then we're all happier.

   B It takes a long time to get used to being rich, so you don't notice if you feel any happier.

   C Money makes us happier if we are richer than those around us, but not if we all have a similar amount of wealth.

b Read the article again and match the missing sentences A–F to the gaps 1–5. There is one sentence you do not need to use.

   A 'People's aspirations tend to rise as their incomes rise, so rather quickly they start to think of a lot of additional things that they need to buy. So they end up no happier than they were before.'

   B Or they are more likely to hold jobs in which people defer to them.

   C The apparent contradiction is that people don't seem to be any happier now than they were then despite their enrichment through economic growth, but that people who are richer at any one time are happier on average than people who are poorer.

   D They think it's important to try to make everyone as happy as they possibly can be.

   E Increase the total amount of happiness, which means enabling people to have better human relationships.'

   F Happiness academics do accept that richer people are, by and large, happier than their poorer neighbours.

c Look at the highlighted expressions and try to work out their meaning. Check in your dictionary.

Does money make you happy?

The unhappy answer to whether or not your happiness expands in line with your wealth is 'yes, but - no, but'. It seems it does if your riches rise relative to that of the Joneses, but not if you all rise together. 'What we actually care about is our income compared with other people,' says Lord Layard, one of the founders of 'happiness studies'. 'But if over time everybody is becoming richer, then people don't on average feel any better than they did before.'

Lord Layard bases the conclusion on studies and surveys that have been conducted over the past half a century or so in the world's richer countries. What the studies reveal is a paradox. ¹____

We like to look out at the neighbours' drive and see a smaller car. This is partly because aspirations rise with incomes. 'You rather quickly get adapted to more money so you don't get the pleasure out of it that you expected to get,' explains Derek Bok, a former president of Harvard University and author of *The Politics of Happiness*. ²____

³____ But they are not even certain that it is the money that does it. 'Happier people on the whole tend to be richer, but we're not quite sure why that is so,' says Mr Bok. 'It may not be the money. It may be that richer people command more respect or they have the freedom to do more things. ⁴____ Or they have more autonomy in what they do. So it

doesn't always follow that giving more money if you don't change those other things is really going to improve their happiness.'

So if money is not all it is cracked up to be, then what should people and governments do? For starters, believes Lord Layard, a break-neck chase after economic growth is misplaced. 'This competition to get richer than other people; it can't be achieved at the level of society,' he says. 'What we should do is have a positive sum. ⁵____

Rather than going for high growth, smoother growth might produce more happiness by producing less disruption and the uncertainty that comes with the ups and down of the economy, according to Lord Layard. 'I certainly think that the relief of poverty is an incredibly important objective, but it shouldn't be done at any cost. We shouldn't just go for economic development even if it leads to the complete fragmentation of society…and a decline in happiness.'

Glossary

The Joneses from the idiom 'keep up with the Joneses', which means to try and have all the possessions and social achievements that your friends and neighbours have.

1 LOOKING AT LANGUAGE

Match a word in **A** to a word in **B** to make compound nouns. Then complete the sentences.

A	age	blood	breathing	college
	life	~~stress~~	support	text

B	exercises	group	~~levels~~	messages
	network	pressure	saver	students

1 My _stress_ _levels_ always go through the roof at exam time.

2 Flu can affect anyone, regardless of which _____ _____ they're in.

3 The doctor has given me some tablets because my _____ _____ is too high.

4 You need your _____ _____ around you to help you through challenging times.

5 Which is cheaper, sending _____ _____ or making phone calls?

6 Pregnant women are encouraged to do _____ _____ to prepare for the birth of their child.

7 A mobile phone can be a _____ _____ if you're involved in an accident and need help.

8 Some _____ _____ suffer badly from stress, particularly at exam time.

2 READING

Read the article. Choose the right answers.

1 Students at Seton Hall...
  a are not allowed to receive visitors.
  b can attend a special programme designed to reduce stress.
  c are allowed to bring their pets to class.

2 The remarkable thing about William Wynne's dog was...
  a it survived for many years on the battlefield.
  b it brightened the atmosphere in the hospital.
  c it made friends with all of the hospital staff.

3 Therapy Dogs International...
  a ensures that animals used for visits are properly trained.
  b works mainly with German Shepherd dogs.
  c raises funds to purchase dogs to use in the organization.

De-stressing with dog therapy

Visitors to Seton Hall University, New Jersey, may be forgiven for thinking they have turned up at the wrong place. Instead of encountering students rushing off to lectures or studying diligently in the library, they will see large numbers of them milling around in a hall in the company of several dogs. But these are no ordinary canines. They are therapy dogs, brought in by the Counselling and Psychology Services Department of the university to de-stress students. And by the looks on the students' faces, the therapy seems to be working.

The first recorded instance of a dog having an impact on our mood occurred during World War II. A soldier, William Wynne, had come across a stray dog on the battlefield that he befriended and named Smoky. Later, when Wynne was admitted to hospital suffering from a tropical disease, his friends took Smoky to visit him. Not only did the animal cheer Wynne up, but it became a big hit with all of the other wounded soldiers on the ward. Noting the positive effect that Smoky had on the men, the doctors allowed the dog to continue doing rounds and sleep on Wynne's bed. Thus Smoky became the first therapy dog, although the term had not yet been coined.

It wasn't until some 30 years later that the concept of therapy dogs really took off. In the mid-1970s, nurse Elaine Smith noticed how well patients responded to a golden retriever brought into hospital by a regular visitor. She decided that there should be more dogs like this in places of healing and so in 1976, she founded Therapy Dogs International, an organization that trained dogs to visit institutions. The first TDI visit took place that year, when five German shepherds and a collie accompanied their handlers to a therapy session in New Jersey. The day was a complete success and since then, TDI has grown to include over 24,000 registered teams of dogs and their handlers.

So how is it that these animals can lead to such a marked improvement in our moods? Research has shown that being around dogs affects various chemicals released by the brain. The amount of the feel-good chemicals, oxytocin and dopamine, increases while the level of stress-inducing substances like cortisol goes down. These variations result in a lowering of the blood pressure, a relief of stress and an improvement in the mood. The dogs experience similar chemical changes as well, and so it's a win-win situation.

The lift in spirits is certainly evident among the students of Seton Hall and other universities with a similar scheme. The students generally reach out and touch the animals as soon as the team from TDI gets through the door. Test-weary faces begin to relax as their worries fade away, and soon everyone is smiling. Of course, the therapy dogs are not able to determine the final grades awarded to the students, but the experience is bound to make the revision process much more bearable.

4 The article describes dog therapy as a 'win-win situation' because...
  a it never fails to work on humans.
  b the handlers benefit as much as the patients.
  c both the patients and the dogs benefit from it.

5 In general, how do students feel about the therapy dogs?
  a They are nervous about touching them.
  b They are eager for them to arrive.
  c They are confident that the dogs will help them.

We cannot change the cards we are dealt,
just how we play the hand.

Randy Pausch, American professor of computer science

6A Change your life!

1 LEXIS IN CONTEXT How to survive...

Look at the Lexis in Context on Student's Book p.54. Then complete the sentences.

1 If you don't **do your sh**_are__ of the housework, we'll have to stop giving you pocket money.
2 Everybody was shocked **beyond b**_____ at the devastation caused by the hurricane.
3 If you feel that you're going to **lose your c**_____ during an argument, it's best to leave the room.
4 Please **h**_____ **in** your key card at the front desk when you depart.
5 My new job is really **st**_____ **me out**. There's too much to do and nobody to help.
6 I don't save a lot of money, but I manage to **sq**_____ **away** a small amount every month.
7 Many medicines should not be taken on an **empty st**_____.
8 Why do you always go into '**child m**_____' whenever we visit your parents? It's the only time you behave in a really immature way!

2 GRAMMAR
verb + object + infinitive or gerund

a (Circle) the right answer.

1 My boss recommended…for the post of supervisor.
   a me applying   (b) me to apply   c me apply
2 Gina's psychologist advised…her routine.
   a her not change   b her not changing   c her not to change
3 Please will you let…the news!
   a me watch   b that I watch   c me to watch
4 Do you remember…you when you were ill?
   a us to visit   b us visit   c us visiting
5 She waited…before phoning her mother.
   a for him leaving   b for him to leave   c him to leave
6 They don't allow…in the reservoir.
   a you to swim   b that you swim   c you swimming
7 We'd like…this gift on behalf of all of us.
   a you to accept   b you accept   c you accepting
8 The doctor kept…for over an hour.
   a me wait   b me waiting   c me to wait

b Complete the sentences with a pronoun and the verb in brackets. Use an infinitive with or without *to* or a gerund.

1 My father-in-law wasn't feeling well so I persuaded _him to seek__ medical help. (seek)
2 A bad experience in Maria's youth taught _____ lies. (not tell)
3 We don't advise _____ with children under 12, though you are welcome to bring teenagers. (come)
4 They're late with the pizzas. We planned for _____ here during half-time. (get)
5 I know you're very good with children, but I can't imagine _____ as a primary school teacher. (work)
6 A special British Airways course helped _____ his fear of flying. (overcome)
7 My friends didn't mind _____ for my drinks last night because they know I'm broke. (not pay)
8 Our visitors are on their way so we'd better hurry home. I'd hate _____ while we were out. (arrive)

3 VOCABULARY compound adjectives

a Complete the compound adjectives.

1 Doctors advise patients with a heart condition not to participate in high-*risk* activities.

2 She's terribly self-_____ about her new haircut; she thinks it's too short.

3 Barbara often goes to charity shops to look for second-_____ clothes.

4 Last-_____ holidays tend to be much cheaper than advance bookings.

5 Our next-door neighbour is a narrow-_____ old man who refuses to listen to new ideas.

b Match a word in **A** to a word in **B** to make compound adjectives, then complete the sentences.

A	dead	eco	feel	ground	hands
	~~high~~	high	labour	life	low

B	breaking	changing	cost	end	free
	friendly	good	~~heeled~~	pitched	saving

1 I'm not used to wearing _high_ - _heeled_ shoes, so I'm going to buy some flat ones.

2 It's a _____ - _____ job – there's no chance he'll ever be promoted.

3 Dogs can hear really _____ - _____ sounds.

4 It's a _____ - _____ movie which makes you realize that life is worth living.

5 Taking a gap year was a _____ - _____ decision for my nephew.

6 We booked with a _____ - _____ airline because the flights were much cheaper.

7 Scientists are using _____ - _____ technology to develop a new treatment for cancer.

8 Washing machines are one of the greatest _____ - _____ devices in the home.

9 They insist on only using _____ - _____ cleaning products so as not to harm the environment.

10 Is it legal to use a _____ - _____ phone when you're driving?

4 PRONUNCIATION main stress

a Underline the main stress in the compound adjectives.

1 <u>air</u>-|con|di|tioned
2 high-|risk
3 home-|made
4 last-|mi|nute
5 long-|dis|tance
6 nar|row-|min|ded
7 se|cond-|hand
8 self-|con|scious
9 well-|be|haved
10 worn-|out

b (iChecker) Listen and check. Then practise saying the words.

5 LISTENING

a (iChecker) Listen to a man suggesting activities to try. Write **S** for summer and **W** for winter next to the activities.

1 Go for a walk _____
2 Learn a new language _____
3 Make a new salad every day _____
4 Run five kilometres _____
5 Start a book club _____
6 Write a blog _____

b Listen again and mark the sentences **T** (true) or **F** (false).

1 The five kilometre app requires one hour of your day for three weeks.

2 A walk in the morning helps start your day in the right way.

3 There are enough salad recipes to be able to eat a different one every day for about a month.

4 The man is no longer a member of a book club as he moved house.

5 According to the man, writing a blog can be time-consuming.

6 The language app only offers a very limited number of languages.

7 The app provides a series of games for a fixed price.

c Listen again with the audio script on p.73 and try to guess the meaning of any words that you don't know. Then check in your dictionary.

6 READING

a Read the article once and tick (✓) the best summary.

1 ☐ Habits are impossible to change, so there's no point in trying.

2 ☐ If you want to change a habit, you first have to understand what causes it.

3 ☐ All habits require the same amount of time to change them.

b Five sentences have been removed from the article. Read it again and match the sentences A–G to the gaps 1–5. There are two sentences you do not need to use.

A Habits are *meant* to be difficult to change.

B It can sometimes be helpful if we imagine that we are someone else.

C This sounds obvious, but countless efforts at habit change ignore its implications.

D Therefore, he reasoned – using the logic we've come to expect from self-help – the same must be true of all big changes.

E So what we really want, it seems, is to stop wanting.

F Either way, it's clear that when you are trying to persuade, how you do it can matter as much as the content.

G Individuals ranged widely – some took 18 days, others 245 – and some habits, unsurprisingly, were harder than others to make stick.

c Look at the highlighted adverbs in the text. What do you think they mean? Check in your dictionary, then use them to complete the sentences.

1 He was found guilty because his crimes could not _____ be blamed on his state of mind.

2 They stared _____ out of the window watching the rain pour down.

3 She's travelled _____ in Australia, so she has a good understanding of the lifestyle and culture.

4 The manager isn't at his desk – _____ he's in a meeting.

5 The system is _____ unfair: the minority has too much to eat while the majority is left to starve.

6 The writer's latest novel is _____ her finest work to date; there is no doubt about it.

CHANGING HABITS:
HOW LONG DOES IT TAKE?

Everyone knows that it takes 28 days to develop a new habit, or perhaps 21, or 18, depending on who you ask; anyway, the point is that it's a specific number, which makes it sound scientific and thus indisputably true. The person who is probably responsible for this idea is Maxwell Maltz, the plastic surgeon who wrote the 1960 bestseller *Psycho-Cybernetics*. He claimed to have observed that amputees took an average of only 21 days to adjust to the loss of a limb. [1]____ . And therefore it must take 21 days to change a habit, maybe, perhaps!

This is, of course, ridiculous, as a new study by the University College London psychologist Phillippa Lally and her colleagues helps confirm. On average, her subjects, who were trying to take up new habits such as eating fruit daily or going jogging, took a depressing 66 days before reporting that the behaviour had become automatic. [2]____ . One especially silly implication of the 28- or 21-day rule is that it is just as easy to start eating a few more apples as it is to start finding five hours a week to study Chinese.

Self-help culture supports the fiction of the 28-day rule, presumably because it makes changing habits sound plausibly difficult enough, but basically easy. The first problem with this is simple: changing habits is hard. Our brains are designed to take short cuts, in order to make as many behaviours as possible automatic. 'What would be the point,' asks the psychologist Ian Newby-Clark, 'of having a habit that didn't free up your mind to deal with more pressing matters?' [3]____

The subtler problem is that we tend to think about habit change wrongly. We get trapped in a paradox. We want to, say, stop watching so much TV, but on the other hand, demonstrably, we also want to watch lots of TV – after all, we keep doing it. [4]____

The way round this, says Newby-Clark and others, is to see that habits are responses to needs. [5]____ If you eat badly, you might resolve to start eating well, but if you're eating burgers and ice cream to feel comforted, relaxed, and happy, trying to replace them with broccoli and carrot juice is like dealing with a leaky bathroom tap by repainting the kitchen. What's required isn't a better diet, but an alternative way to feel comforted and relaxed. 'The chains of habit are too weak to be felt until they are too strong to be broken,' Dr Johnson observed gloomily, but maybe by looking at the problem differently we can still, Houdini-like, slip out of them.

Cell phones are so convenient that they're an inconvenience.

Haruki Murakami, Japanese author

6B Can't give it up

1 VOCABULARY phones and technology

a Complete the words.

1 I need to **m**_ake_ a call. Can I borrow your phone?
2 Is there a socket? I need to **ch**_____ my phone.
3 I'll be at home so call me on the **l**_____ .
4 I can't get a **s**_____ here, can you? There's really bad coverage.
5 I'll **g**_____ you a call this evening when I'm home.
6 She's very busy so her phone is often **e**_____ .
7 Please leave a message after the **t**_____ .
8 Can you repeat that? The **r**_____ isn't very good here.
9 I've got six **m**_____ calls from Jake. I hope nothing's happened to him.

b Circle the correct particle.

1 I've forgotten my password, so I can't log _____ .
   (a) in   b out   c up
2 I usually top _____ my credit about once a month.
   a in   b on   c up
3 We were cut _____ when the train went through a tunnel.
   a down   b off   c out
4 You can never get _____ after ten, so call early.
   a in   b on   c through
5 How can I free _____ some space on this pen drive?
   a up   b out   c off
6 Her secretary won't put _____ any calls if she's busy.
   a across   b through   c along
7 She didn't want to talk to him so she hung _____ .
   a off   b out   c up
8 Scroll _____ the page to find the answer.
   a down   b on   c in
9 The battery has run _____ , so I can't use my phone.
   a off   b out   c over
10 Can you speak _____ ? It's very loud in here.
   a in   b out   c up

c Circle the correct word.

1 A *cookie* / *virus* is a file that is capable of causing damage to your computer.
2 *Wi-fi* / *Broadband* is a technology that uses radio waves to allow you to connect to the internet.
3 A *keypad* / *keyboard* is the set of numbers usually found on a phone.
4 *Streaming* / *Downloading* does not allow you to save any data on your computer.
5 A *password* / *passcode* is the set of numbers that unlocks your phone, for example.
6 *An update* / *A pop-up* is a piece of free software which is sent to users to fix or improve a computer program.
7 Your *contacts* / *settings* is where your friends' numbers can be found.
8 A *screen* / *touch screen* is one that can be controlled with a pen or a finger.

2 LEXIS IN CONTEXT Without a mobile phone, you basically don't exist

Look at the Lexis in Context on Student's Book p.59. Then complete the sentences.

| albeit | decent | donned | justification |
| negotiation | plausibility | ~~untenable~~ | wolf |

1 The lawyer refused their case because he said it was _untenable_ .
2 We had worked together before, _____ only for a short time.
3 My teenage kids usually _____ their lunch when they get home from school.
4 There was no _____ for his behaviour and he was forced to apologize.
5 For Andrew, it was beyond the realms of _____ that Clara didn't want to marry him.
6 When it was discovered that the politician had been lying, he did the _____ thing and resigned from his post immediately.
7 Their proposal was not a firm arrangement but a basis for _____ .
8 He put on his coat, _____ his hat, and left the house.

3 PRONUNCIATION /æ/ and /ʌ/

a **iChecker** Listen and circle the word you hear.

1	a bag	b (bug)	6	a ban	b bun
2	a sank	b sunk	7	a cap	b cup
3	a hat	b hut	8	a drag	b drug
4	a slam	b slum	9	a fan	b fun
5	a rat	b rut	10	a lamp	b lump

b Practise saying both words in each pair.

4 GRAMMAR conditional sentences

a Complete the sentences with a suitable form of the verb in brackets.

1 If Simon _didn't have_ such a demanding job, he wouldn't get so stressed. (have)

2 You _____ to use your mobile unless you charge the battery first. (not be able)

3 I wouldn't have woken you up if you _____. (not snore)

4 If you _____ to class yesterday, you won't know about the next exam. (not come)

5 _____ you _____ your car more often if you could afford it? (change)

6 We'd be starving by now if we _____ something before we left home. (not eat)

7 Lily _____ us by now if she wasn't having a good time. (call)

8 We _____ the bank so much money now if we hadn't asked for such a big mortgage. (not owe)

b Rewrite the sentences using the **bold** word.

1 I'll lend you some money if you pay me back. **long**
I'll lend you some money _as long as you pay me back_ .

2 We didn't know you were at home, otherwise we would have called in. **had**
_____ ,
we would have called in.

3 What would you do if you missed your flight? **supposing**
_____ ?

4 I'm not going away with my parents this year, even if they don't like it. **whether**
I'm not going away with my parents this year,
_____ .

5 You can borrow my bike if you look after it. **provided**
_____ , you can borrow it.

6 We'll have to get a new sofa, whether we can afford it or not. **even**
We'll have to get a new sofa, _____ .

7 If Sarah finishes the report by the weekend, she can have Monday off. **condition**
Sarah can have Monday off _____ .

8 We said the children could stay up if they didn't make too much noise. **as**
We said the children could stay up _____ .

5 VOCABULARY adjectives + prepositions

Match the sentence halves and write the missing preposition in the gap.

1 His parents are very proud | e |
2 Many people are fed up | |
3 New Yorkers are generally helpful | |
4 Full-time housewives may be dependent | |
5 My sister is obsessed | |
6 They said they were open | |
7 Many people are not keen | |

a _____ the idea of negotiating the contract.

b _____ fashion magazines and buys two or three a week.

c _____ self-catering because they don't like having to cook on holiday.

d _____ tourists.

e _of_ his achievements at university.

f _____ their spouses financially.

g _____ the depressing stories in the news recently.

6 LISTENING

a **iChecker** Listen to five people talking about obsessions. What are they obsessed with or addicted to?

1 _____
2 _____
3 _____
4 _____
5 _____

b Listen again and answer with the number of the speaker.

Who...?

A ☐ says that they would be even more obsessed if it weren't for their family

B ☐ doesn't really think that they are obsessive

C ☐ wasn't aware of the damage an obsession could cause

D ☐ doesn't think that the obsession serves any purpose

E ☐ says that the obsession started because of a family member

c Listen again with the audio script on p.73 and try to guess the meaning of any words that you don't know. Then check in your dictionary.

7 READING

a Match the apps to the functions, then read the article once to check the answers.

1 ☐ Venmo   a getting a taxi
2 ☐ Instagram   b finding a partner
3 ☐ Tinder   c making payments
4 ☐ Uber   d sending messages
5 ☐ Waze   e sharing photos
6 ☐ WhatsApp   f getting directions

Six apps we couldn't live without

A few years ago, the most popular apps were casually addictive games that provided us with entertainment during our daily commute. Now there is a whole new generation of them that are influencing our offline life more and more each day. Here is a list of six of the apps we couldn't possibly live without today.

A **Venmo** Venmo is a free app that allows you to exchange payments with people you know via your smartphone, linking to your Facebook friends and email contacts, as well as your bank. Opt to give someone enough trust and they can withdraw money directly from your account, through the app. You can also build up a pile of cash in your Venmo account, so that next time you head out to dinner with friends, it's fairly easy to split the bill or pay someone back.

B **Instagram** When it comes to sharing photos through our phones, most people prefer Instagram, the app bought by Facebook for $1 billion in late 2012. With 150 million monthly active users sharing 16 billion photos a day, Instagram has added a feature that gives users more control over who sees their photos. Instead of posting a photo to your entire network, you can send it to between one and 15 people, preventing strangers from viewing your pics without your knowledge.

C **Tinder** This matchmaking app lets users trawl through photos of other singles on their smartphone, swiping the ones they like to the right and those they don't to the left. If two people swipe each other to the right, Tinder notifies them of their 'match'. Tinder is reportedly used by more than one per cent of the population in some countries and it has been suggested that the kids of the future will ask their parents which app they met in.

b Read the article again and choose the correct answer from the apps A–F. The apps may be chosen more than once.

Which app…?

1 ☐ has caused a conflict with an existing business
2 ☐ offers a service created using content from its users
3 ☐ has a component that helps protect a user's privacy
4 ☐ sends users a message when two things coincide
5 ☐ would only be used among the most honest of friends
6 ☐ do long-term users have to pay for
7 ☐ appeals to users because it makes international communication cheaper
8 ☐ only works in cities
9 ☐ requires users to categorize images
10 ☐ necessitates the involvement of an external organization
11 ☐ can facilitate your daily commute
12 ☐ allows users to select who can see their activity

c Look at the highlighted verbs and match them to the definitions below. Write the verbs in the infinitive.

1 search through a large amount of information
_____
2 follow the movements of something _____
3 make something change direction _____
4 cause to work together _____
5 divide _____
6 move the fingers across a touch screen _____
7 upload something onto a web page _____
8 take money from an account _____

D **Uber** Uber is a car-for-hire app that finds a driver within your area and, assuming you're in a metropolis, can often send it to your doorstep within minutes. It was named tech company of the year in 2013 because of the changes it was likely to bring to our lives. Since then, however, transport authorities have accused the company of operating an illegal taxi service, and legal action has been threatened.

E **Waze** This was the first app to successfully build up an enormous databank of maps and traffic reports through crowdsourcing. Waze has succeeded in creating a highly accurate navigation service by tracking the GPS coordinates of its users. It also diverts them away from built-up traffic when enough of them report in that they're stuck in a jam.

F **WhatsApp** WhatsApp was the first of the messaging apps to offer a free texting service that synched with your mobile number and address book so that you didn't have to register with a username. Founded in 2009, it now has 400 million active users to whom it charges a minimal annual subscription after one free year. The app's main advantage is that it can be used to avoid expensive texting charges when communicating with friends and colleagues overseas.

7A Quite interesting

1 PRONUNCIATION
intonation and linking in exclamations

a **iChecker** Listen and tick (✓) the phrases where the words are linked with a /w/ sound.

1 How awful! ✓	5 How ridiculous!
2 How fantastic!	6 How unkind!
3 How exciting!	7 How brilliant!
4 How wonderful!	8 How weird!

b Practise saying the exclamations, copying the rhythm and intonation.

c Draw a line between the words that are linked.

1 What‿an‿absolute disaster!
2 What a tragic end!
3 What a nice surprise!
4 What a sad ending!
5 What an awful thing to happen!
6 What a horrible story!
7 What a lovely day!

d **iChecker** Listen and check. Practise saying the exclamations, copying the rhythm and intonation.

2 VOCABULARY word formation: prefixes

a Complete the sentences with a word from the list with a negative prefix.

competent	continued	hospitable	literate
official	personal	~~practical~~	rational

1 High-heeled shoes are *impractical* for walking long distances.
2 The climate on that island is so _____ that nothing can live there.
3 Adults who were _____ used to sign their name with a cross.
4 He's very upset, so his behaviour may be _____.
5 I refuse to go that restaurant again because the staff are completely _____.
6 I can't get new parts for my car because they've _____ that model.
7 I hate big hotel chains because they are so _____.
8 Rumour has it that she's going to resign, but the reports are _____.

b Add the prefixes from the list to the **bold** words and make any other necessary changes to complete the sentences.

anti	de	ill	~~mis~~	out
over	pre	re	under	up

1 I completely _*misunderstood*_ the instructions and I answered two questions instead of one. **understand**
2 Many countries have passed _____ laws because of the rise in tobacco-related illnesses. **smoke**
3 We'll never go to back to that hotel. They tried to _____ us on our bill by £60. **charge**
4 I _____ my Facebook status yesterday, but no one has commented on it. **date**
5 Since many people are unable to attend today's meeting, it has been _____ for next Tuesday. **schedule**
6 My boss's negative attitude to everything is very _____ for the staff. **motivate**
7 The other team completely _____ us and we lost 6–0. **play**
8 My mother's hair became _____ grey when she was only 35. **mature**
9 He lost a lot of money because of the _____ investments he made. **advise**
10 The organizers _____ how many people would attend, so there weren't enough chairs. **estimate**

3 LEXIS IN CONTEXT
It's health and safety gone mad!

Look at the Lexis in Context on Student's Book p.67. Then complete the sentences with the past simple forms of the verbs.

~~ban~~	beep	calm	cite	confiscate	grimace
impose	interfere	limp	reinforce		

1 They _banned_ teenagers wearing hoodies from the shopping centre because they couldn't be identified.
2 My grandmother _____ into the room, supporting herself on her walking stick.
3 We went to the town hall to protest when the council _____ the new parking restrictions.
4 The teacher _____ my mobile phone because I was playing with it in class.
5 She _____ her heavy workload as the reason for her resignation.
6 The recent loss to Italy _____ my belief that England will not qualify for the next World Cup.
7 When we first moved in, our neighbour's Wi-fi _____ with ours.
8 The player _____ in pain when the doctor touched his swollen ankle.
9 The new road design _____ the traffic by giving pedestrians and cyclists priority.
10 There was very little damage because the smoke detector _____ as soon as the fire started.

4 GRAMMAR
permission, obligation, and necessity

a ~~Cross out~~ the modal verb that is NOT possible in the sentences.

1 *We need to | We've got to | We can* check out before 12, or the hotel will charge us for another night.
2 When we were children, we *couldn't | shouldn't | weren't allowed to* stay out late.
3 I *should have | must have | ought to have* packed some warmer clothes – I'm freezing!
4 You *mustn't | aren't supposed to | don't have to* walk dogs on this beach, but many people do.
5 Some members of my family *couldn't | needn't | weren't able to* attend our wedding because it was held abroad.
6 I *mustn't | needn't | don't have to* study tonight because my exams are over.
7 *We ought to | We're allowed to | We'd better* look in on your mother this weekend. She hasn't been well.
8 We *didn't need to | didn't have to | couldn't* ring the bell because the door was open.
9 You *can | should | ought to* see a doctor about that cough.

b Rewrite the sentences using the **bold** words.

1 It is compulsory for motorcyclists to wear a helmet. **to**
You _have to wear a helmet_ on a motorbike.
2 We regret buying such a big house. **shouldn't**
We _____ such a big house.
3 I couldn't wear jeans to work in my previous company. **wasn't**
I _____ jeans to work in my previous job.
4 Our teacher says we should always speak English in class, but not all of us do. **are**
We _____ in class, but not all of us do.
5 Don't be late. The class always starts on time. **better**
You _____ late. The class always starts on time.
6 We're going on holiday so we can't come to your wedding. **won't**
We _____ to your wedding as we're going on holiday.
7 The best thing to do would be to apply for a transfer to a different department. **to**
You really _____ for a transfer to a different department.
8 We took sandwiches, but they weren't necessary. **taken**
We _____ sandwiches.
9 You cannot use mobile phones in this carriage. **It**
_____ mobile phones in this carriage.

5 LISTENING

a **iChecker** Listen to an interview with Anna Usborne, ex-pupil of a Steiner School. In general, does she regard her education as a positive experience, a negative experience, or both positive and negative?

b Listen again and mark the sentences **T** (true) or **F** (false).

1 Steiner Schools focus on the needs of the child rather than imparting information.
2 Anna was not required to take any exams while she was at school.
3 Today, she would not be permitted to travel to school in the way that she did in the past.
4 She has very fond memories of her early school years because she was free to do what she wanted.
5 She considers that she learnt more about art at her school than she would have at any other.
6 She regards the primary stage of her education as much more effective than the secondary stage.

c Listen again with the audio script on p.73 and try to guess the meaning of any words that you don't know. Then check in your dictionary.

6 READING

a Read the article and match the headings A–F with the stories 1–4. There are two headings you do not need to use.

A Forbidden flowers
B Too near the ground
C The end of sweets
D No celebrating
E No more experiments
F Putting your foot in it

b Complete the article with **a**, **b**, or **c**.

1 a but
   b or
   c neither

2 a therefore
   b as
   c although

3 a However
   b Actually
   c Otherwise

4 a According to
   b As regards
   c Despite

5 a must
   b can't
   c couldn't

6 a definitely
   b continually
   c unlikely

7 a don't
   b do
   c didn't

8 a So
   b Besides
   c Though

c Look at the highlighted words and expressions and match them to the synonyms below.

1 careful

_____

2 showing the opposite

_____

3 a set of laws

_____

4 in use

_____

5 who has a position of power

_____

Debunking health and safety myths

In the UK, it is the Health and Safety Executive that is responsible for passing legislation aimed at keeping the population safe. While many of the rules and regulations currently in effect have indeed been issued by this organization, a number of myths abound. Here are some of the worst of them.

1 ____
Each year we hear of companies banning employees from decorating their offices at Christmas for 'health and safety' reasons, ¹____ requiring the work to be done by a 'qualified' person. Such rules have never been issued by the Health and Safety Executive, ²____ managers would be sensible to provide staff with step ladders to hang up decorations rather than expecting them to balance on wheelie chairs.

2 ____
Back in 2004, a town did briefly take down its hanging baskets over fears that old lamp posts would collapse. This was an excessively cautious reaction to a low risk. ³____, after quick checks, the hanging baskets were promptly replaced and have been on lamp posts in the town every year since. ⁴____ this, the story continues to be repeated and the danger is that someone in authority will believe it and take action.

3 ____
The idea that park benches ⁵____ be replaced because they are 8 cm too low seems to have originated from a decision by one particular park manager; it has no basis in health and safety law at all. There are no such bench height requirements and inspectors will ⁶____ not be sent around measuring the benches at any point in the near future.

4 ____
Despite recent reports to the contrary, health and safety law does not ban staff from wearing sandals or flip-flops at work. It must be said, however, that slips, trips and falls ⁷____ account for about 30 per cent of all workplace accidents. ⁸____, if you work somewhere where the floor can't be kept dry or clean, then wearing shoes that fit well and have a good grip would be a better choice than flip-flops.

It is not hard to understand modern art. If it hangs on a wall it's a painting, and if you can walk around it it's a sculpture.

Tom Stoppard, British playwright

7B A beautiful idea

1 GRAMMAR verbs of the senses

a Complete the sentences with a suitable form of a verb from the list.

hear	look	not feel	not sound
see	seem	smell	~~taste~~

1 I was told this was duck, but it __*tastes*__ like chicken.
2 We _____ your family last weekend – do we have to go again so soon?
3 Rob, I _____ just _____ that you're leaving the company. Is it true?
4 Urgh! It _____ as if someone has been smoking in the lift.
5 Can we put the heating on? It _____ very warm in here.
6 When my son was born, he _____ exactly like my father.
7 You _____ very well. Have you got a sore throat?
8 The shop assistant _____ to be ignoring us. Let's go somewhere else.

b Rewrite the sentences using the **bold** words.

1 I don't think those players are very fit. **look**
   Those players __*don't look*__ very fit.
2 Look! That waiter just dropped a tray full of glasses. **see**
   Did you _____ a tray full of glasses?
3 It looks as if that man has lost something. **seems**
   That man _____ something.
4 I don't think that noise is a police siren. **sound**
   That noise _____ a police siren.
5 My cousin Rachel is the image of my aunt. **exactly**
   My cousin Rachel _____ my aunt.
6 The baby was crying. John went to pick her up. **heard**
   John _____, so he went to pick her up.
7 We appear to be heading in the wrong direction. **as**
   It _____ heading in the wrong direction.
8 I can hear someone upstairs. **like**
   It _____ there's someone upstairs.
9 It smells like something's burning. **smell**
   I _____ burning.

2 PRONUNCIATION -ure

a (Circle) the word in which *-ure* is pronounced differently.

1 cap**ture** plea**sure** (se**cure**)
2 end**ure** mea**sure** pic**ture**
3 all**ure** cul**ture** fu**ture**
4 imp**ure** na**ture** obsc**ure**
5 lei**sure** sculp**ture** **sure**
6 furni**ture** imma**ture** tempera**ture**

b [iChecker] Listen and check. Practise saying the words.

3 VOCABULARY art

Complete the crossword.

Clues across →

1 a painting that expresses the artist's ideas of people or things and is not a realistic representation
5 a painting of an artist by the artist him / herself
6 a painting of a view of the countryside

Clues down ↓

2 a figure or object made from wood, stone, etc.
3 a painting of a person
4 a painting of flowers or fruit arranged on a table

4 LEXIS IN CONTEXT

The Secret of *The Forest*

Look at the Lexis in Context on Student's Book p.71. Then complete the time expression verbs.

1 The gallery is currently being refurbished, but the work is due to finish **by** the end of the year.
2 The exhibition opens in a **c**_____ of hours, so let's have lunch and then come back.
3 They married in 2005, and about a year **l**_____ they had their first child.
4 Fortunately, the thief was caught **w**_____ days of the robbery, when he tried to sell the stolen paintings to another gallery.
5 Rhythm and blues music didn't become popular **u**_____ the Fifties.
6 The performer was able to memorize a pack of playing cards in just a **f**_____ minutes. It was really amazing to watch.

5 VOCABULARY colour idioms

Complete the sentences with a colour idiom containing the word in **bold**.

1 The new multi-storey car park is an expensive _white elephant_; nobody uses it. **white**
2 The artist's comment had nothing to do with the real interpretation of the picture; it was a _____ _____. **red**
3 Nobody knew that she was thinking of leaving, so her resignation came _____ _____ _____ _____. **blue**
4 Some people see politics _____ _____ _____ _____, but most situations aren't that simple. **black**
5 The taxation of online companies is a _____ _____, as it isn't clear where the money should be paid. **grey**
6 You have to deal with a lot of _____ _____ if you want to set up your own business, but there are lots of experts to help you. **red**
7 He was arrested for buying and selling stolen goods on the _____ _____. **black**
8 I don't really like her paintings at all, but I told her a _____ _____ so as not to hurt her feelings. She's quite sensitive! **white**

6 LISTENING

a **iChecker** Listen to a radio programme about Vladimir Tretchikoff's painting *The Chinese Girl*. Who did better as a result of the painting, the artist or the model?

b Listen again and answer the questions.

1 How old was Monika Pon-su-san when she modelled for the painting?
2 Where exactly was Monika when she met Tretchikoff?
3 Had she heard of him before? Why?
4 What is the difference between the gown Monika was wearing and the one in the painting?
5 What did Monika think about while Tretchikoff was painting her?
6 How much did Tretchikoff pay Monika for modelling for him?
7 What didn't she like about the painting?
8 What happened to Monika after her encounter with Tretchikoff?
9 How did Monika feel when she heard the price the painting fetched at auction?

c Listen again with the audio script on p.74 and try to guess the meaning of any words that you don't know. Then check in your dictionary.

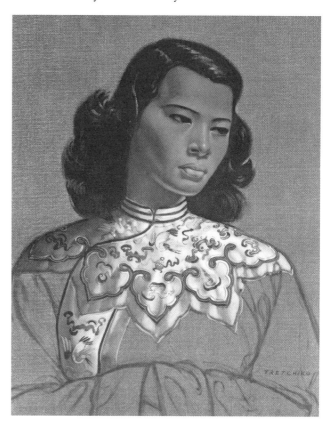

7 READING

a Read the article once and tick (✓) the best title.

1 The life and works of Henri Matisse ☐
2 Five stars for Matisse's cut-outs ☐
3 Art award for London gallery ☐

b Five sentences and paragraphs have been removed from the article. Read it again and match A–F to the gaps 1–5. There is one sentence or paragraph you do not need to use.

A For the cut-outs were never planned, as such. Matisse developed them late in life not as an end in itself, but as a working method for trying out different compositional and colour arrangements for the illustrations to his book *Jazz* (1943–46). As he realized the importance of what he had done, the cut-outs evolved into a new art form.

B In the process, new compositions were created. The works that now give us so much pleasure are a step removed from the ones that Matisse made.

C What makes the exhibition outstanding is that the curators have placed Matisse's creative process at its heart. Starting with the works of art as they exist today, they go back in time to look at the methods and materials he used at each stage in their transformation from the raw materials of paint, paper, and scissors to the dazzling result before us.

D Today, when we look at *Oceania, the Sea* (1946) Matisse's representation of a silent, silvery underwater world teeming with unconventional sharks and jellyfish, coral and starfish, we marvel at the elegance of white shapes placed on a soft beige-coloured canvas edged with lapping waves. But can you imagine if those shapes moved ever so slightly as we passed in front of them?

E Matisse had long been interested in the theme of the artist's studio and the decorative interior. But an even more direct forerunner of the astonishing rooms we see in photographs of his studio in Nice in the early 1950s is *Harmony in Red*, a painting of 1908 now in the Hermitage.

F The use of pins meant that the bits of paper could be moved or rotated as the artist wished. In one of the larger cut-outs, for example, conservation scientists have counted as many as 1,000 pin pricks, indicating that Matisse must have drastically altered the composition as he worked.

c Look at the highlighted verbs and try to work out their meaning. Check in your dictionary.

Tate Modern must know that with 'Matisse: the Cut-Outs' they have a winner. I guarantee that this exhibition of the colour-saturated works Henri Matisse made by cutting out shapes from pre-painted sheets of paper during the last 17 years of his life will be among the most popular ever held in the UK.

1_____ The joy of the cut-outs is their simplicity. They are made out of modest materials using basic techniques, and in them Matisse reduces art to the essentials of colour, shape, and pattern. Yet precisely because they offer us instant visual gratification, it is easy to forget how innovative they actually are.

2_____ The process starts by cutting out shapes from sheets of paper that have already been painted in colours chosen by the artist. These cut-out shapes are then pinned (but not glued) to a support, which might be a sheet of paper, a wall, or a canvas. 3_____

Because the shapes of palm leaves, mermaids, parrots, and coral reefs were not fixed permanently to a flat surface, the cut-outs are much more physical than mediums such as painting and collage. It changes your understanding to learn that in their original form they might flutter slightly in a breeze, gaining a sense of movement.

4_____ Matisse could only use pins during the first phases of his work. Of necessity, the next step had to be to glue the paper shapes to the support in order to preserve it. For purely practical reasons, then, Matisse had the cut-out shapes taken off the wall, traced, and glued onto canvas.

5_____ So congratulations are in order for the curators of Tate Modern. Their beautifully realized exhibition changes our understanding of what Matisse achieved in the cut-outs. From now on we'll see them not simply as delightful arrangements of shapes and colours, but as works of art that represent the grand finale of an artistic genius.

Colloquial English Talking about...illustration

1 LOOKING AT LANGUAGE *get*

Complete the *get* expressions with the words in the list.

age   kind   mood   number
~~published~~   way   work

1 Roald Dahl got his first children's book _*published*_ in 1943.
2 I was taking a photo of the view when somebody got in the _____ .
3 You might get the printer to _____ better if you clean it.
4 You get a different _____ of look if you use pastel colours.
5 If you like him, why don't you just get his _____ and give him a call?
6 I hope to have saved enough money by the time I get to retirement _____ .
7 We put on some music to get in the _____ for the party.

2 READING

a Read the article and answer the questions.

1 Why has the art world taken an interest in Anna and Elena Balbusso?
2 At which point in their lives did they go their separate ways?
3 Why did they decide to start working together again?
4 What is special about the works published by the Folio Society?
5 What is the function of a 'handmaid' in the novel *The Handmaid's Tale*?
6 What appealed to Anna and Elena most about the novel?
7 What are the most striking features of their illustrations for the novel?
8 Which prize did their illustration *Pregnant* win?

b Underline five words or phrases you don't know. Use your dictionary to look up their meaning and pronunciation.

Anna+Elena=Balbusso

In the solitude of the studio, the lone artist hunches over a canvas to add the final brush strokes to a portrait. Or at least that is how these professionals are commonly perceived. Yet a pair of Italian sisters has recently debunked this myth by producing a series of strikingly beautiful pictures as a team. It may help that illustrators Anna and Elena Balbusso are identical twins, and the fact that they are able to create such perfect works as a duo has got the art world talking.

The sisters began drawing together as children, when they would get hold of pencils and coloured markers and cover sheets of squared notebook paper with pictures. They drew their way through primary school and after secondary school, they were lucky enough to both attend a special high school that was dedicated to art: the Instituto Statale d'Arte in their hometown, Udine. After both gained their diplomas, they went on to specialize in painting and art history at the Academy of Fine Arts of Brera in Milan.

At this point in their careers, the sisters decided to branch out on their own, and spent the summers working separately as graphic designers with studios and advertising agencies in Milan. Upon graduation, they had intended to continue this path but a crisis in advertising and graphics meant that there was little work available. Consequently they decided to return to the medium of their youth – drawing – and independently began to visit publishing houses in Milan. Soon, however, the editors began to comment on how confusing it was to first receive one sister with her portfolio and then an hour later the other. To avoid the confusion, the sisters created a single identity and since 1998, they have been working together under the signature *Anna+Elena=Balbusso*.

During the years of their partnership, the sisters have been rewarded with a number of commissions, including several from the prestigious Folio Society, a privately-owned publisher which produces special hardback editions of classic fiction and non-fiction books illustrated by professional artists. Undoubtedly one of their greatest works to date has been their award-winning illustrations of Margaret Atwood's classic novel *The Handmaid's Tale*. Set in the future in the fictional Republic of Gilead, where women have lost all of their rights and are only valued for their ability to reproduce, the story explores the fate of Offred, a 'handmaid' employed by a military commander and his wife to bear children for them.

The two sisters were the perfect choice for this particular book, not only because of their talent, but also because their own story is reflected in the main character's struggle to find and maintain her own identity in a circle dominated by men. To create the right atmosphere, they chose a futuristic tone with accentuated perspectives and strong light. They used few colours, with a prevalence of red, black and white. The result was a series of haunting images that emphasize the alienation of the main character and reflect the regimented society in which she lives. The Balbusso sisters' picture *Pregnant* from the series was chosen by the Society of Illustrators as the best illustration of 2012 and awarded a gold medal. Which only goes to show that in the world of art, sometimes two heads can be better than one.

8A Doctor's orders

1 VOCABULARY health and medicine

a Complete the puzzle to discover the hidden word.

1 A strip of cloth used for tying around the injured part of a person's body to protect or support it.
2 Become unconscious when not enough blood is going to your brain.
3 A special photograph that shows bones or organs in the body.
4 A doctor who is trained to perform operations.
5 A medical test in which a picture of the inside of a person's body is sent to a computer screen.
6 A common illness affecting the nose and throat that makes you cough and sneeze.
7 A piece of material that can be stuck to the skin to protect a wound or a small cut.
8 A purple mark that appears on the skin if you fall or are hit by something.
9 A medical condition of the chest that makes breathing difficult.

Hidden word: _____

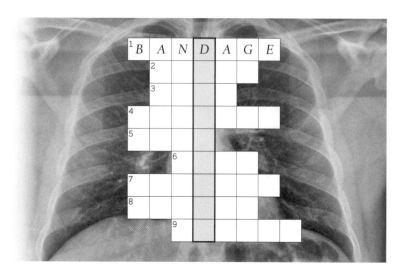

b Complete the words.

1 Peter's GP sent him to a heart **sp**_ecialist_ to find out what was causing the pain in his chest.
2 I didn't dry my hands before unplugging my phone charger, so I got an **e**_____ **sh**_____.
3 I got a **bl**_____ on my little toe when I wore my new trainers.
4 My girlfriend hasn't had seafood since she had an **a**_____ **r**_____ after eating some prawns on holiday one time.
5 I thought I had a cold, but when I got a temperature, I realized it must be **fl**_____.
6 The doctor prescribed **a**_____ to clear up my throat infection.
7 Matt had eight **st**_____ in his eyebrow when he cut it playing rugby.
8 My grandfather was told to take it easy after he had his first **h**_____ **a**_____.
9 My son must be allergic to eggs because he comes out in a **r**_____ every time he eats them.
10 Alex is in bed with a nasty bout of **f**_____ **p**_____ after eating some mayonnaise that was off.

2 LEXIS IN CONTEXT
What doctors won't do...

Look at the Lexis in Context on Student's Book p.74. Then complete the sentences.

1 When it comes to living longer, not everyone would agree that the advantages outweigh the **d**_isadvantages_.
2 My reluctance to use Botox has **n**_____ to do with the cost; it's the fact that it's a highly poisonous substance that worries me.
3 People underestimate the **r**_____ of self-medicating; you could be taking some tablets with harmful side-effects while the real problem is getting worse.
4 It makes a doctor's **h**_____ sink when whole families make one appointment during which they all expect to be seen.
5 Don't take my **w**_____ for it – read this article. It says that honey and lemon is the best cure for a cough.

3 GRAMMAR gerunds and infinitives

a Complete the sentences with the correct gerund or infinitive form of the verbs in the list.

become	complain	~~forget~~	learn	photograph
programme	set up	sniff	take	wear

1 Ryan apologized for *having forgotten* my name the day before.
2 My parents never record TV programmes because they don't know how _____ their DVD player to record in advance.
3 You seem _____ a lot at the moment. Have you got a cold?
4 Many celebrities say they are fed up with _____ every time they leave the house.
5 It's no good _____ about your back. Why don't you make an appointment to see the doctor?
6 What was the last animal _____ extinct?
7 Eve would rather _____ a new outfit to the wedding last week, but she couldn't afford one.
8 There's no point in _____ antibiotics if you've got a virus.
9 A couple I know had a plan _____ their own business, but it fell through when they split up.
10 _____ several languages before, I'm finding my new course quite easy.

b Complete the sentences with three words. Use the correct gerund or infinitive form of the verbs in brackets.

1 I would thoroughly recommend this resort to families with young children. There is plenty for *them to do* . (do)
2 We hope _____ off the mortgage on our house by the time we retire. (pay)
3 I would love _____ my paternal grandfather, but he died before I was born. (meet)
4 Our holiday in the French Riviera was a bit of a disappointment because it wasn't warm _____ in the sea. (swim)
5 How frustrating for them _____ the match in the last minute! They must have been gutted. (lose)
6 It is very common for employees _____ redundant when their company is doing badly. (make)
7 A friend of mine is hoping _____ for a TV cookery show. (choose)
8 Most children enjoy _____ the zoo by their parents. (take)
9 _____ book first really helped me to understand the plot in the film. (read)
10 There's _____ in our village in the evenings – not even a pub. (go)
11 There's _____ your sister to the wedding. We know she won't come. (invite)

4 LEXIS IN CONTEXT Medical advice

Look at the Lexis in Context on Student's Book p.77. Complete the sentences with the correct form of *make* or *do*.

1 I can't _*make*_ up my mind whether to have surgery to correct my eyesight or not.
2 Adam's wife is the one who _____ the decisions in their relationship.
3 Can using herbal remedies _____ you any harm?
4 If everybody recycled their household waste, it would really _____ a difference.
5 Doctors say that a brisk walk _____ you good if you spend most of the day sitting down.
6 He _____ the recommended warm-up exercises, but he still managed to injure himself.
7 _____ friends is easier when you're young because you're usually surrounded by your peers.

5 VOCABULARY similes

Complete the sentences with a verb or adjective.

1 We've just bought a new laser printer. It _*works*_ **like a dream**.
2 My boyfriend is **as** _____ **as a mule**. He refuses to stop the car and ask for directions.
3 What's wrong? You've gone **as** _____ **as a sheet**!
4 My new dog is **as** _____ **as gold**. It never bites or chews the furniture.
5 Your uncle _____ **like a fish**. Is he an alcoholic?
6 I dropped my knife and **as** _____ **as a flash** the waiter brought me a new one.
7 I usually _____ **like a log**, but yesterday I had a really bad night.
8 Alice is **as** _____ **as a rake**. I don't know how she manages it considering how much she eats!
9 Our neighbour always has the TV on really loud. He's **as** _____ **as a post**.
10 The waiter's walked straight past us several times. He must be **as** _____ **as a bat**.

6 PRONUNCIATION /ə/

a **iChecker** Listen to the sentences and circle the unstressed words with the /ə/ sound.

1 The treatment cost a lot more than we'd thought.
2 The surgeon arrived as soon as the patient was ready.
3 It was too late for a doctor, so we went straight to hospital.
4 The specialist suggested I went on a diet for a while.
5 I'm allergic to plasters, so I never use them.

b Look at the stressed words in **a** and underline any syllables with the /ə/ sound.

c Practise saying the sentences.

7 READING

a Read the article once. Which phrase do you think is missing from the title?

1 If all else fails, try homeopathy
2 Homeopathy kills
3 Steer clear of homeopathy

say scientists

Homeopathy, the alternative therapy created in 1796 by Samuel Hahnemann, and now widely used all over the world, is based on the belief that the body can be stimulated to heal itself. A central principle of the 'treatment' is that 'like cures like' – in other words, a substance that causes certain symptoms can also help to remove those symptoms. Medicines used in homeopathy are created by heavily diluting in water the substance in question and subsequently shaking the liquid vigorously. They can then be made into tablets and pills. Practitioners believe that the more a substance is diluted in this way, the greater its power to treat symptoms.

However, in a new study, a working committee of medical experts at Australia's National Health and Medical Research Council (NHMRC) has claimed that homeopathic medicines are only as effective as placebos at treating illnesses. Their research, involving the analysis of numerous reports from homeopathy interest groups and the public, concluded that there is no reliable evidence that homeopathy works. Moreover, researchers uncovered no fewer than 68 ailments that homeopathic remedies had failed to treat, including asthma, sleep disturbances, colds and flu, burns, and arthritis.

As a result of the findings, the NHMRC is urging health workers to inform their patients to be wary of anecdotal evidence that appears to support the effectiveness of homeopathic medicine. 'It is not possible to tell whether a health treatment is effective or not simply by considering the experience of one individual or the beliefs of a health practitioner,' says the report. Experts believe that most illnesses said to have been cured by homeopathy would be cured by the body on its own without taking the medicine. Apparently, many illnesses are short-lived by their very nature which often leads to people believing that it is the homeopathy that cures them.

A more serious matter is highlighted by Professor John Dwyer of the University of New South Wales. As an immunologist, he is concerned about the homeopathic vaccinations on offer for diseases such as HIV, tuberculosis, and malaria, none of which he considers effective. According to Professor Dwyer, the concept that homeopathic vaccinations are just as good as traditional vaccinations is a delusion, and those who believe it are failing to protect themselves and their children.

b Read the article again and choose the best answers.

1 According to the article, homeopathic medicines are… .
   a prepared in the same way
   b made up of many ingredients
   c suitable for a wide range of symptoms
   d available only in liquid form

2 The Australian study reveals that homeopathy is… .
   a extremely popular with the public
   b helpful in the case of respiratory infections
   c ineffective in treating many illnesses
   d only of interest to certain groups of people

3 People tend to believe in homeopathy because of… .
   a adverts displayed in health centres
   b positive feedback from a small number of people
   c advice they get from the medical profession
   d the results of research into alternative therapies

4 In Professor John Dwyer's view, homeopathic vaccinations are… .
   a not worth bothering with
   b often harmful
   c ridiculously expensive
   d better than nothing

c Look at the highlighted words and phrases connected with health and medicine and try to work out what they mean. Check in your dictionary.

8 LISTENING

a (iChecker) Listen to a radio programme about American teenager, Ashlyn Blocker. What are the symptoms of her medical condition and what is its cause?

b Listen again and mark the sentences **T** (true) or **F** (false).

1 Ashlyn's condition isn't life-threatening.
2 She sometimes hurts herself when she is making a meal.
3 When she was born, her behaviour wasn't normal.
4 Doctors diagnosed her condition when she was around two years old.
5 The staff at her school weren't very co-operative.
6 When she was a child, her parents managed to prevent her from hurting herself.
7 Publicity has helped her cause immensely.
8 Her condition has been caused by an alteration in more than one of her genes.

c Listen again with the audio script on p.74 and try to guess the meaning of any words that you don't know. Then check in your dictionary.

The world is a book and those who do not travel read only one page.

Augustine of Hippo, early Christian theologian

8B Traveller or tourist?

1 VOCABULARY travel and tourism

a Complete the verbs.

1 During her trip to Kenya, Becky w_ent___ on a safari.
2 We had to c_____ our holiday when my husband lost his job – we just couldn't afford it.
3 We're going to the mountains for the weekend to g_____ away from it all.
4 They're going to p_____ their honeymoon until the bride's mother has had her operation.
5 I prefer to w_____ round the sites on my own rather then listening to a tour guide.
6 We decided to e_____ our stay by two nights because we were having such a good time.
7 They s_____ off early to avoid the traffic.
8 We're broke this year, so we're going to g_____ camping instead of staying in a hotel.
9 As soon as we'd checked into the hotel, we made for the city centre to h_____ the shops.
10 If you're feeling tired, perhaps you should take a few weeks off to r_____ your batteries.
11 The best thing about going abroad is being able to s_____ the local cuisine.
12 For me, the main aim of a holiday is to ch_____ out and forget about work for a while.
13 You need to spend at least a week in Venice to really s_____ up the atmosphere.

b Replace the **bold** words and phrases with the words and phrases in the list.

breathtaking	dull	lively	off the beaten track
overcrowded	overrated	picturesque	remote
spoilt	tacky	~~touristy~~	unspoilt

1 The town is full of hotels and shops; it's too **designed to attract visitors** for me. _touristy_
2 Some of our coastal areas have been totally **changed for the worse** by over-development. _____
3 There's no Wi-fi signal because the village is very **far from places where other people live**. _____
4 Don't bother going into that shop; all of the souvenirs are very **cheap and badly made**. _____
5 There are some beaches in the north which are **beautiful because they have not been changed**. _____
6 Our holiday was quite **boring** last year – nothing interesting happened. _____

7 Ibiza is a **vibrant** island, famous for its nightlife and parties. _____
8 I think the Seaview Hotel is **not nearly as good as the reviews said** – we were very disappointed. _____
9 Torremolinos in southern Spain is no longer the **old-fashioned, pretty** little fishing village it was in the 1950s. _____
10 We rarely go to the beach in August because it's always **too full of people**. _____
11 When we eventually reached the top of the mountain, the view was **absolutely spectacular**. _____
12 We wanted to rent a quiet cottage **away from where people normally go**. _____

2 LEXIS IN CONTEXT
Are you a tourist or a traveller?

Can you remember the phrasal verbs from the article on Student's Book p.79? Choose the right answer.

1 The town…a tourist destination when the latest season of a popular TV series was filmed there.
   a turned out   (b) turned into   c turned on
2 The guests…in horror as the fire swept through the hotel.
   a looked on   b looked out   c looked down on
3 They had to cancel the excursion because the coach didn't… .
   a turn up   b turn in   c turn off
4 Stop…how much we've spent; we've all had a great time and that's all that matters.
   a going ahead with   b going after   c going on about
5 The boy…at a distance from his parents, hoping that nobody would realize they were together.
   a stood up   b stood off   c stood up to
6 She…her husband's relations, who she considered inferior to her own family.
   a looked up to   b looked over   c looked down on
7 I was…, so I thought I'd stop and say hello.
   a passing over   b passing away
   c passing through
8 I…an old friend at the market, so we went and had a coffee together.
   a ran over   b ran into   c ran out of

3 GRAMMAR
expressing future plans and arrangements

a Circle the correct form. Tick (✓) if both are possible.

1 From now on, I'm *going to save* | *about to save* my money instead of spending it all on clothes.

2 Our plane *takes off* | *is taking off* in three quarters of an hour.

3 Sylvia is so disillusioned with her course that she's *due to leave* | *on the point of leaving* university.

4 *Do you eat* | *Will you be eating* in the hotel restaurant tonight, sir?

5 My nephew *is due to start* | *is starting* university in September.

6 *I won't be driving* | *I'm not to drive* to work next week because my car will be at the garage.

7 The neighbours have invited us round tonight because they're *having* | *going to have* a party.

8 The Royal Family *are to visit* | *are going to visit* the Netherlands, Belgium, and Germany next month.

9 Sorry, but *I'm about to go* | *I go* into a meeting. Can I call you back in half an hour?

b Complete the second sentence so that it means the same as the first using the **bold** words.

1 Anna intends to have an early night tonight. **is**
Anna _is_ _going_ _to_ _have_ an early night tonight.

2 We expect the flight to land in about ten minutes. **due**
The flight _____ _____ _____ _____ in about ten minutes.

3 May I ask who is picking me up from the station? **be**
Who _____ _____ _____ _____ _____ from the station?

4 The managing director is about to retire. **point**
The managing director is _____ _____ _____ _____ retiring.

5 I'm catching the 12.15 bus to Seville tomorrow. **at**
My bus to Seville _____ _____ 12.15 tomorrow.

6 The play is going to start very soon. **about**
The play _____ _____ _____ _____ .

7 I have arranged to take part in a half-marathon next Saturday. **taking**
I _____ _____ _____ in a half-marathon next Saturday.

8 They are going to hold the general election on March 3rd. **to**
The general election _____ _____ _____ _____ on March 3rd.

4 LEXIS IN CONTEXT
Christmas getaway crippled by storms

Look at the Lexis in Context on Student's Book p.80. Then complete the sentences.

1 The plane looked as if it was going to land, but then it **sh**_ot_ back up in the air.

2 The captain said the lights would be switched back on when we had gained sufficient **h**_____ .

3 It was quite stormy when we flew to Dublin, so the flight was rather **b**_____ .

4 After such a long delay, the passengers were **r**_____ when they boarded the plane at last.

5 We flew into thick cloud as we were **a**_____ Heathrow.

6 The plane **c**_____ the airport until the pilot was given permission to land.

7 My parents are **o**_____ to Greece tomorrow and are really excited.

8 We were advised to keep our seatbelts fastened in case we hit some **t**_____ .

9 The flight arrived so late that we faced the **d**_____ of whether to spend the night in the airport or pay for a taxi to the city centre.

10 The gale-force **w**_____ on the coast caused serious damage last night.

5 PRONUNCIATION homophones

iChecker Listen to the sentences and circle the right spelling of the words you hear in the sentence.

1	a board	b bored	6	a brake	b break
2	a caught	b court	7	a sight	b site
3	a fair	b fare	8	a peace	b piece
4	a key	b quay	9	a suite	b sweet
5	a wait	b weight	10	a cereal	b serial

6 READING

a Read the article once and tick (✓) the best summary.

1 ☐ Career breaks to travel are usually amazing experiences, but you may put your job at risk.

2 ☐ Career breaks to travel sound like a good idea, but are often not worth it.

3 ☐ Most people who take career breaks to travel do not regret their decision.

The truth about taking a career break to travel

They say that travel broadens the mind, an adage which implies that the more we see of the world, the better. Yet once we get a foot on the career ladder, most of us put this idea to the back of our minds. ¹_____ But does taking a break to travel really have such a negative effect on your career?

Diving enthusiast Russ Brooks found that it did not. When he was 36, Russ took a career break of 11 months which took him to 16 different countries. ²_____ 'The break showed that I was an independent thinker and willing to take risks to succeed,' he says. 'Nothing like a few stories of travelling in the developing world to show you can cope with anyone and any situation.' Contrary to what our society says, Russ was indeed employable.

Not only was Russ successful in his job hunt, but the break helped him to get his career back on the right track. 'My time away gave me time to unplug and recharge, see the world in an incredibly different light,' he says. 'It allowed me the time to step back and think about what was truly important to me. When I returned, I was inspired not to settle until I had found work that matched my core values.' ³_____

Far from having a negative impact on your career, taking a break to travel can actually increase your prospects when presented in the right way. Heather Baker, an HR professional in Chicago, advises on how to best explain the time away. 'Think about this from the employer's point of view. ⁴_____ Include it on your CV and share the details of when and why you did the break, as well as the result. If you are enthusiastic and positive about the experience, your passion will shine through and excite your potential employers as well.'

The main reason why travel improves a person's job prospects is that it can help them stand out in a crowd. ⁵_____ Mitchel Samuelson was surprised by his interview experiences after the six months he spent travelling. 'All the companies I interviewed with, the first topic we discussed was my career break and travelling, as it was either a common interest or they were envious and/or interested in where I'd gone.'

To sum up, then, it appears that the consequences of taking a career break to travel are nothing but positive. These breaks often provide people with better opportunities on their return, and on top of that, they can lead to more clarity and job satisfaction. ⁶_____ So, now that you know that travelling will not destroy your career, you can start planning your next career break. Bon voyage!

b Read the article again and match the missing sentences A–H to the gaps 1–6. There are two sentences you do not need to use.

> A On his return, it only took him three or four months to find employment.
>
> B As a side benefit, it allows you to see the world before you retire.
>
> C Long-term travel emphasizes a person's uniqueness and lets them be noticed – in a good way.
>
> D Most people cite fear of change, financial concerns, and lack of stability as excuses not to quit their job and head out to see the world.
>
> E In many cases they don't know what they want, so they stay.
>
> F After his sense of community was re-energized during his career break, Russ came back to become the CEO of a social impact media company.
>
> G We all fantasize about it: quitting our jobs, hopping on a plane, and heading out to see the world.
>
> H They want to know your career path and how this career break fits into that.

c Look at the highlighted words and phrases and try to work out their meaning. Check in your dictionary.

7 LISTENING

a **iChecker** Listen to Moira, who lives in the USA, describing a disastrous journey. How long did it take her to get home? Tick (✔) the right answer.

1 eight hours ☐
2 twelve hours ☐
3 fourteen hours ☐
4 three days ☐

b Listen again and answer the questions.

1 What was unusual about the weather that day?
2 How far is Moira's home from her office?
3 Who offered to give Moira a lift home?
4 Why had so many drivers parked at the side of the road?
5 What were some of the people walking along the road wearing?
6 What problems did they have between 5.30 and 6.45 a.m.?
7 Where did Moira tell the driver to drop her off?
8 Where did Moira walk to avoid falling over?
9 How did Moira get down the hill leading to her house?
10 What time was it when Moira eventually got home?

c Listen again with the audio script on p.75 and try to guess the meaning of any words that you don't know. Then check in your dictionary.

The greatness of a nation and its moral progress can be judged by the way its animals are treated.

Mahatma Gandhi, Indian spiritual leader

1 LEXIS IN CONTEXT
In defence of not liking animals

Look at the Lexis in Context on Student's Book p.85. Then complete the sentences with a verb or adjective from the list.

| adores | ~~averse~~ | care | content | live | sceptical |

1 My girlfriend says she loves animals, but she's not _averse_ to eating them!
2 My aunt _____ cats; she's got six of them.
3 I am _____ to have a cat in the house, so long as it doesn't scratch the furniture.
4 Unfortunately there are people who _____ very little about how farm animals are treated.
5 At first I was _____ about eating tofu, but now I've decided that I quite like it.
6 My son wants a turtle. I can _____ with that, as long as he agrees to clean the tank every week.

2 VOCABULARY animal matters

a Complete the puzzle to discover the hidden word.

1 A young sheep.
2 The noise made by a mouse.
3 The noise made by a horse.
4 The hard outer part of a snail.
5 A young hen.
6 Young cows.
7 The place where a canary is kept.
8 The sharp curved nails on the end of a lion's paw.
Hidden word: _____

b (Circle) the word that is different. What animal do the other three words describe?

1 foal   hooves   (roar)   stable   _horse_
2 bark   horns   kennel   puppy   _____
3 fur   nest   twitter   wings   _____
4 beak   kitten   meow   paws   _____
5 fins   grunt   tail   tank   _____
6 grunt   hooves   tail   twitter   _____

c Complete the sentences.

1 In some countries, veal calves are kept in **in**_humane_ _conditions_ in wooden crates where they cannot turn around.
2 Zoos today obtain animals **br**_____ in **c**_____, instead of catching them in the wild.
3 When the cosmetics testing laboratory opened, animal **r**_____ **a**_____ gathered outside the building to protest.
4 In many countries, rabbits and deer are **h**_____ for **sp**_____.
5 Orang-utans are one of the most **en**_____ **sp**_____ in the world.
6 The World Wildlife Fund is a **ch**_____ which aims to **pr**_____ animals and the **en**_____.
7 Wolves used to **l**_____ in the **w**_____ in most of Europe.
8 In the past, animals were sometimes **tr**_____ **cr**_____ in circuses.

3 GRAMMAR ellipsis

a Match the sentence halves. Tick (✓) the sentences where you don't need to repeat *they* in a–i.

1 They tried the soup, but [f] [✓]
2 The men were whistling while
3 They'll have to get a visa before
4 The neighbours were green with envy when
5 They hurried to the gate and
6 The kids were moaning because
7 They chatted for a while, and then
8 They only realized the painting was a fake after
9 My parents either have lunch at home or

a they saw our beautiful new car.

b they had bought it.

c they turned off the light and went to sleep.

d they worked.

e they can travel there.

f ~~they didn't like it.~~

g they boarded the plane.

h they eat out.

i they didn't want to do their homework.

b (Circle) the correct modal or auxiliary verb.

1 Dan hasn't been camping before, but his friends *do* | *(have)* | *were*.

2 My brother said he wasn't coming on holiday with us this year, but I think he *was* | *might* | *does*.

3 Very few people in my street recycle their rubbish, but we always *are* | *will* | *do*.

4 I know you haven't apologized yet, but I really think you *did* | *should* | *have*.

5 Everyone said I'd win the prize, but I knew I *wouldn't* | *haven't* | *didn't*.

6 They thought they'd be able to come to our wedding but, in fact, they *wouldn't* | *couldn't* | *shouldn't*.

7 Jessica gives the impression of being very confident, but actually she *can't* | *isn't* | *wasn't*.

8 Most people weren't paying attention, but Andy *did* | *was* | *has*.

9 My best friend said she'd come clubbing with me tonight, but now she says she *wouldn't* | *hadn't* | *won't*.

c Complete the mini-dialogues with a suitable word.

1 **A** Will we be going away in August as usual?
   B I imagine _so_. Unless something comes up.

2 **A** I suppose we should get on with our work.
   B I guess _____. The deadline is in two days.

3 **A** Will you be joining us for dinner on Sunday?
   B We'd like _____, but we can't.

4 **A** Do you think you'll get a pay rise this year?
   B I suspect _____. We made a big loss last year.

5 **A** Will your parents be at home this evening?
   B I assume _____. They don't usually go out.

6 **A** Why did you buy that hideous green hat?
   B My friend persuaded me _____.

7 **A** Can I have a refund for this coat, please?
   B I'm afraid _____. We only give refunds for non-sale goods.

8 **A** Did you report the incident to the police?
   B No, our lawyer advised us not _____.

4 PRONUNCIATION auxiliary verbs and *to*

a Read the dialogue and under<u>line</u> the auxiliaries or *to* when you think they are stressed.

   A Do you know where you're going on holiday yet?
   B No, I <u>don't</u>. I'd love to go on a safari, but my girlfriend doesn't want to.
   A She doesn't like animals, does she?
   B She does like animals – she's got three cats. But she doesn't want to go on a safari.
   A Where does she want to go, then? Doesn't she want to see lions in the wild? I'd love to.
   B So would I. And so would my girlfriend. But she really doesn't like camping. Neither do I if I'm honest.

b **iChecker** Listen and check. Practise the dialogue.

5 LISTENING

a **iChecker** Listen to five people talking about how they are similar to their pets. Match the speakers to five of the animals in the box.

cat	dog	goldfish	horse
lizard	mouse	parrot	rabbit

1 Speaker 1 _____
2 Speaker 2 _____
3 Speaker 3 _____
4 Speaker 4 _____
5 Speaker 5 _____

b Listen again and answer the questions. Write the number of the speaker.

Which speaker...?

A ☐ says that they and their pet have developed simultaneously

B ☐ likes the way their pet behaves towards another person

C ☐ believes that having a pet has changed them

D ☐ thinks that pets' personalities change according to the owners they have had

E ☐ admits they have gestures that they picked up from their pet

c Listen again with the audio script on p.75 and try to guess the meaning of any words that you don't know. Then check in your dictionary.

6 READING

a Read the article once. Which of these benefits of having a pet are NOT mentioned in the text?

1 They oblige their owners to do exercise.

2 They protect their owners from burglars.

3 They help owners get over the death of a partner.

4 They can help elderly owners who are disabled.

5 They motivate their owners to look after themselves.

6 They provide an opportunity to make friends.

b Five sentences have been removed from the article. Read it again and match the sentences A–F to the gaps 1–5. There is one sentence you do not need to use.

A Among 200 subjects, she found that symptoms of distress including uncontrolled tearfulness and feelings of hopelessness and helplessness were all lowered among pet owners.

B There are strong economic reasons for us as a society to do our best to encourage old people to keep pets.

C The benefits of animal companionship for older people are now well documented; it is the practicalities that often prove the stumbling block.

D Self-care is often tied in with pet care, which is especially important for those who live alone.'

E His name is Ollie, he came to them after the death of his 81-year-old owner and they already 'love him to pieces'.

F We have no way of knowing whether animals are actually sympathetic, but they respond to changes in behaviour and body language in a way that gives comfort.

c Look at the highlighted words and phrases. What do you think they mean? Check in your dictionary.

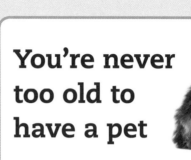

You're never too old to have a pet

When Anthony and Jacqueline Rich's Yorkshire terrier Monty died last November at the age of 14, the couple, who are in their sixties and have had dogs for four decades of married life, were devastated. Today there is another Yorkie at their home in Looe, Cornwall. [1] _____ It is a simple enough equation — bereaved owner plus bereaved pet equals comfort and new joy for both parties — but one that could hold the key to much human and animal happiness.

[2] _____ This month Dr June McNicholas, a health psychologist and senior research fellow at Warwick University, will embark on a study which aims to identify those factors that may prevent the elderly from keeping pets and which suggests possible solutions.

'Old people with pets are generally more active and alert,' she says. 'Obviously, walking a dog is good exercise and can also be a way of preserving social contacts or making new friendships, but even just getting up and down to see to the cat or going to the shops for food is better than nothing. Research has also found that those who have animals tend to keep their homes warmer in winter and to feed themselves more regularly. [3] _____

In an earlier project McNicholas studied the role of animals in helping people widowed after long marriages. [4] _____

McNicholas says: 'In the early stages the animal was a continuing link with the loved one. The bereaved often want to talk about the person they've lost, but other people don't, so instead they talk to the dog, which responds to the name. One woman told me, 'When I want to talk, I talk to my daughter; when I need to cry, I cry with my dog.' [5] _____ So in a way it doesn't matter whether it is real, it feels real.

If your mother cooks Italian food,
why should you go to a restaurant?

Martin Scorsese, American director

9B How to eat out...and in

1 VOCABULARY preparing food

a Circle the correct answers.

1 Have you ever tried (baked) | melted | scrambled figs with gorgonzola cheese?

2 We always make cheese on toast with boiled | chopped | sliced bread.

3 She only wanted a snack for lunch, so she had a barbecued | poached | toasted sandwich.

4 Sprinkle a little chopped | roast | sliced parsley over the potatoes before serving.

5 I'll have apple pie with baked | stewed | whipped cream for dessert.

6 We're having mashed | melted | scrambled eggs and bacon for breakfast.

7 You'll need some grated | minced | stuffed beef if you're making spaghetti bolognese for dinner.

8 He really loves having deep-fried | poached | whipped onion rings for a starter.

9 My favourite seafood dish is steamed | mashed | toasted mussels.

10 They're both trying to lose weight, so they ordered grilled | minced | peeled fish.

b Write the names of the kitchen equipment in the picture.

1 _kettle_   6 _____
2 _____   7 _____
3 _____   8 _____
4 _____   9 _____
5 _____   10 _____

2 PRONUNCIATION
words with silent syllables

a ~~Cross out~~ the vowels which are **not** pronounced in the words.

1 interesting   5 temperature
2 comfortable   6 chocolate
3 medicine   7 dictionary
4 different   8 vegetables

b **iChecker** Listen and check. Practise saying the words.

3 LEXIS IN CONTEXT How to eat out

Look at the Lexis in Context on Student's Book p.89. Then complete the words and phrases.

chew	fiddly	~~fuss~~	gobble	stuff

1 I hate going for dinner with Linda; she's always making a _fuss_ about something.

2 Most of the things I cook are quite simple; I can't be bothered with dishes that are very _____.

3 I've got no idea what to order; there's far too much _____ on the menu.

4 My teenage sons are usually starving, so they _____ up their food in a matter of seconds.

5 My dog eats so quickly, I swear she doesn't actually _____.

4 GRAMMAR nouns: compound and possessive forms

a Right (✓) or wrong (✗)? Correct any mistakes in the highlighted phrases.

1 I opened the front door because I thought I'd heard the bell ring. ✓

2 Matt put his sunglasses in the handbag of his girlfriend. ✗ _his girlfriend's handbag_

3 We're going to spend a fortnight at my parents' villa on the coast. _____

4 Sebastian is the son of the neighbour you met yesterday. _____

5 My mother is hopeless at buying men's clothes, so my father always buys his own. _____

6 Please remember to put your bowl of cereal in the dishwasher after breakfast. _____

7 She's a language assistant at a private secondary school. _____

8 What happened at the story's end? _____

9 The supermarket has stopped giving away free bags of plastic. _____

10 We went round to Heather's last night.
_____

b Complete the sentences with a word from **A** and a word from **B**. Add 's, s', or ' where necessary.

A	alarm	animal	bread	Fiona and Charles
	~~guest~~	husband	trainee	vegetable	women

B	cages	car	clock	clothes	drawer
	~~house~~	knife	magazines	manager

1 They found a cheap _guest house_ where they could spend the night.

2 Sarah doesn't know much about current affairs because she only reads _____ for fashion tips and celebrity news.

3 Please can you put the carrots and beans in the _____ in the fridge?

4 _____ was seriously damaged in the crash.

5 After school, my brother went to work for a bank as a _____.

6 Lily is fed up with finding her _____ all over their bedroom floor. She's going to talk to him about it later.

7 Don't use the _____ to cut meat.

8 In most zoos, the _____ aren't as small as they used to be.

9 My _____ didn't go off, so I was late for work.

5 LEXIS IN CONTEXT Well-known faces reveal their ultimate comfort food

Look at the Lexis in Context on Student's Book p.91. Then complete the sentences.

1 C_andy_ is the American English word for sweets.

2 Ch_____ are small green or red peppers that are used in cooking to give a hot taste to food.

3 G_____ is the root of a plant of the same name which is used in cooking as a spice.

4 M_____ is a rather ugly fish which is said to taste like lobster.

5 O_____ are large flat shellfish.

6 LISTENING

a **iChecker** Listen to three people describing cooking disasters. Were any of them able to eat what they cooked?

b Listen again and complete the chart.

1 Who were they cooking for?		
Speaker 1	Speaker 2	Speaker 3

2 What were they making?		
Speaker 1	Speaker 2	Speaker 3

3 What went wrong?		
Speaker 1	Speaker 2	Speaker 3

4 What happened in the end?		
Speaker 1	Speaker 2	Speaker 3

c Listen again with the audio script on p.76 and try to guess the meaning of any words that you don't know. Then check in your dictionary.

7 READING

a Read the article once and tick (✓) the best alternative heading.

1 Where to eat out in London
2 Sourcing ingredients for the perfect dish
3 The changing tastes of the British
4 Eat well; be healthy

b Read the article again and choose **a**, **b**, **c**, or **d**.

1 In the first paragraph, the writer expresses surprise at… .
   a the current reputation of British cooking
   b British people's aversion to eating raw food
   c how quickly British people's tastes have changed
   d British people's ignorance of foreign dishes

2 According to the writer, in the past, British tourists abroad were renowned for… .
   a sampling the local cuisine
   b often bringing their own food with them
   c arguing with waiters about the quality of the food
   d refusing to eat any bread

3 In the third paragraph, the writer criticizes the British food of the past because… .
   a it always looked the same
   b it always involved the same ingredients
   c it was always cooked in the same way
   d it always tasted the same

4 The stories in the fourth paragraph illustrate that when new food products became available in the 1970s in Britain, people… .
   a didn't want to try them
   b didn't like the look of them
   c didn't know how to prepare them
   d thought they were ridiculously overpriced

5 According to the writer, with the expansion of international travel, the British have become more interested in… .
   a eating out
   b having more professional service
   c how healthy their food is
   d where their food comes from

6 The writer concludes that the British today are… .
   a trying out more recipes
   b showing more interest in food
   c relying more on traditional ingredients
   d spending more time on food shopping

c Look at the highlighted words and phrases and try to work out their meaning. Check in your dictionary.

Glossary

sliced white a loaf of white bread that is sold already cut into slices

---

The joy of fine food

As London toasts itself as the world's most exciting gastronomic city, it is amazing to remember just how recently it was catapulted to the top table. Even 30 years ago, most Britons presented with a plate of salmon sushi would have sent it back to the kitchen and wondered what possessed the chef to send out the fish so obviously undercooked. Steak tartare, ditto. A Caesar salad? That would presumably have been something that Roman emperors ate.

Yes, you could get something that called itself a curry in most towns. Also sweet-and-sour pork. Italian restaurants still carried an air of exoticism, with their waiters waving pepper mills the size of baseball bats. The stereotypical British holidaymaker abroad was one who, when offered garlic bread would shriek, 'What? Garlic bread? Garlic? Bread? Am I hearin' you right? Garlic bread? No, thank you, I've got some sliced white in my case; that'll do me.'

'Tell me what you eat,' said the French gastronome Jean-Anthelme Brillat-Savarin, 'and I will tell you what you are.' Even two or three decades after the end of the war, when the rigour of rationing was losing its grip, Britons must have been beige. Because the food they ate came in shades of brown, long before paint manufacturers made that a fashionable colour palette.

As recently as 1974, retailers were handing out leaflets explaining that while an avocado pear might sound like a fruit, it was best eaten with lemon juice or vinaigrette. 'Don't approach a courgette with fear and trepidation,' it urged. 'For your first attempt at cooking them, simply simmer in salted boiling water.' Dentists must have been able to afford second homes after the introduction of pistachios: so many customers tried to eat them with their shells that eating instructions eventually had to be included.

As travel and trade across Europe became freer, as cheaper air fares brought America and Asia within tourist budgets, British palates grew more adventurous and discerning. Where once it was hard to get a good cup of coffee, now coffee-drinkers demand their beans come not just from a particular country, but from a specific coffee bush. Visit a restaurant today and the waiter will mention, as if it mattered, that the salt on the table is sourced from the Himalayas and the pepper from Madagascar.

The kitchen has become the heart of the middle-class home. Cookery programmes continue to captivate TV audiences, even if we watch them while waiting for our Thai green curry ready-meal in the microwave to ping. Cookbooks are the only books that many people buy. Recipes in newspapers include ingredients that, three decades ago, would have required new trade routes to be introduced to facilitate their import. Now, no supermarket could survive that stocked only one type of tomato. In short, we have become a nation of gourmets celebrating the joy of fine food.

1 LOOKING AT LANGUAGE
informal and vague language

bit	going	like	pretty	so
something	there	went	~~whatever~~	whole

Complete the informal and vague language in the sentences with the words in the list.

1 We usually have a quick lunch: a salad or a sandwich or **wh**_atever_.

2 Ants can be a **b**_____ of a pain when you're camping.

3 I opened a box of chocolates last night and my husband ate the **wh**_____ lot!

4 I was **l**_____, 'Please don't let that be mine!' when the waiter brought our meals.

5 I'm **pr**_____ sure that I've never eaten an insect.

6 Cattle farming will probably die out in the next hundred or **s**_____ years.

7 Matt **w**_____, 'What is _that_?' when he saw dim sum for the first time.

8 There are loads of people out **th**_____ who don't know the meaning of a balanced diet.

9 My kids are always **g**_____, 'I don't like this. Can I have that?'

10 There are **s**_____ like 4,500 species of cockroaches in the world.

2 READING

a Read the article and mark the sentences **T** (true) or **F** (false).

1 Camren fed his mealworm dinner to canaries.

2 He was disgusted by the idea of eating insects until fairly recently.

3 He mixes the insects with everyday ingredients.

4 All of the dishes he's tried on the diet have been a hit.

5 He used the same supplier as many zoos to get the insects he needed for his diet.

6 He is not expecting a quick change in attitudes.

b Under<u>line</u> five words or phrases you don't know. Use your dictionary to look up their meaning and pronunciation.

Anyone for a bug-burger?

US student Camren Brantley-Rios is clearing away the dinner dishes. Nothing unusual, you might think, until you find out what he has just eaten. On tonight's menu was fried rice with mealworms – the larva stage of an insect that is usually fed to canaries. What Camren did was to season the mealworms with soy sauce and add them to the rice he was frying. Apparently, the concoction tasted pretty good.

Camren hasn't always had such a strange diet. In fact, he used to be one of the many Americans who find the idea of eating grubs and insects quite repulsive. That is, until he realized how much damage consuming traditional meats is doing to the environment. It has been discovered that keeping livestock, such as cattle, causes unacceptably high emissions of greenhouse gases, such as methane and ammonia. At the same time, insects consume fewer resources than cows to produce a similar amount of protein: there are 19 g of protein in 100 g of meat, while the same weight of grasshoppers contains 13 g. Seeing that the current meat industry is unsustainable, Camren decided to try out what could be the food of the future: a bug diet. Since then, 30 days have passed, and Camren has been eating insects three times a day: for breakfast, lunch, and dinner.

Mealworms are just one of the species he's been ingesting. Together with waxworms and crickets, these form the bulk of his diet. Everyday meals include scrambled eggs with waxworms, bug-burgers with cheese, and creole crickets, a dish with an extra-spicy sauce. Every so often, he tries to incorporate something different into his cooking – with varying degrees of success. He got a pleasant surprise as a result of sautéing orange-spotted cockroaches with herbs, mushrooms and onions, but was unable to finish the dish he had prepared with silkworm pupae because of its unpleasant smell.

According to the UN Food and Agriculture Organization, more than two billion people worldwide include insects in their regular diet, but this does not mean they are readily available for purchasing in the US. For this reason, Camren has had to turn to the internet to find his ingredients. The insects he procures have been fed on an organic diet, and he only buys species he knows are safe to eat. One of his main suppliers is a farm that supplies zoos with bugs to feed to reptiles. Once Camren has placed an order, the insects are sent to him by post.

Camren is fully aware that one person eating insects won't have a real environmental impact and that it would take millions of people following his example to make a difference. Right now, however, this is unlikely as there is not much pressure for Americans to eat bugs because of the finer meats still available, albeit at a cost. What Camren hopes is that eating insects will become a little more marketable in the future, so that people will slowly come round to the idea. Meanwhile, his experiment is having an unexpected effect on the people around him, as some of his friends are asking him to cook for them. Perhaps in the not-so-distant future, we may all be having bug-burgers for dinner.

Remember, remember always, that all of us, and you and I especially,
are descended from immigrants and revolutionists.

Franklin D. Roosevelt, American president

10A Where do I belong?

1 LEXIS IN CONTEXT
Interview with David and Emma Illsley

Look at the Lexis in Context on Student's Book p.95.
Then complete the sentences with idioms and phrasal
verbs.

1 I've always **had a h**<u>*ankering*</u> to live by the sea, so we've
been looking at properties on the coast.
2 We **r**_____ **out** the possibility of going to China
because it was too expensive.
3 She **turned her b**_____ **on** her parents when
they needed her, claiming that she was too busy to help.
4 Treating his injuries was one thing, but getting him to
walk again was **a bigger h**_____ .
5 My father let me have his old car for **next to
n**_____ .
6 If you need some **consumer d**_____ , go to the
Scottish Highlands; you won't see a shop for miles.
7 As we were walking through the countryside, we
st_____ **on** the ruins of a castle.
8 My niece **had a b**_____ during her first year of
university; it was one big party.

2 GRAMMAR adding emphasis (2): cleft sentences

a Match the sentence halves.

1 It was the shellfish | *h*
2 All I want
3 The reason why you weren't invited
4 What happened
5 All I did
6 The day I moved into my new house
7 What happens
8 The thing I admire most about him

a was say what I thought.
b was when I first met Miranda.
c is that you order and pay at the bar, and then we bring
the food to your table.
d is a bit of sympathy.
e is his determination to enjoy life.
f was that we took the wrong turning off the motorway.
g is that you'd said you'd be away.
h ~~that made everybody ill.~~

b Rewrite the sentences to give them extra emphasis,
starting with the word(s) given.

1 She just wanted to apologize.
All <u>*she wanted was to apologize*</u> .
2 I spoke to the assistant manager, not the manager.
The person _____ .
3 I didn't buy the bag because it was too expensive.
The reason _____ .
4 Her grandmother taught her how to bake bread.
It _____ .
5 Jane shut the door with her keys still inside.
What happened _____ .
6 I need a good, long rest.
What _____ .
7 I was impressed by how quickly she learnt Italian.
The thing _____ .
8 My parents live in a very picturesque village.
The village _____ .

3 PRONUNCIATION
intonation in cleft sentences

a **iChecker** Listen and write the sentences.

1 _____
2 _____
3 _____
4 _____
5 _____
6 _____

b Practise saying the sentences.

4 LEXIS IN CONTEXT
Tea and sandwiches with the Queen

Look at the Lexis in Context on Student's Book p.97. Then complete the sentences with the formal words.

acquiring	dispiriting	entered	gravely	melancholy
on	~~primary~~	proceedings	reflecting	seek

1 His _primary_ concern is his family, not his career.
2 _____ returning home, they discovered that their house had been burgled.
3 The gallery is in the process of _____ an original Picasso.
4 He seemed completely uninterested in the _____ and appeared to fall asleep.
5 It was a bit _____ to see our team defeated last season in every match they played.
6 The psychiatrist nodded _____ as the patient explained his problem.
7 Everyone went quiet when the speaker _____ the room.
8 I often find myself _____ on what would have happened had I followed a different career path.
9 You should _____ advice from a lawyer if you have any doubts about your rights.
10 I am always overcome by a feeling of _____ when the summer is over.

5 VOCABULARY
words that are often confused

a Circle the correct word.

1 The company is going to advertise / announce the vacancy in the local newspaper.
2 The next time my brother asks me for a loan, I'm going to refuse / deny.
3 Monica feels a bit dizzy, so she's gone to lie / lay down for a while.
4 I suppose I'll get married one day, but right now I'm not ready to make a compromise / commitment.
5 Some people say that gas is more economic / economical than electricity, but I'm not so sure.
6 We were delighted with our suit / suite – it had a balcony with a hot tub.
7 Let's eat out tonight. I'm starving and, beside / besides, I don't fancy cooking.
8 The actress is actually / currently dating her bodyguard after her marriage broke up last year.
9 She was extremely ashamed / embarrassed when her trousers ripped as she sat down.
10 Global warming affects / effects the world's weather in many ways.

b Complete the sentences with the words you didn't circle in a.

1 The managing director is going to _announce_ his retirement at the next board meeting.
2 We sat on the grass _____ the river and had a picnic on Saturday – it was idyllic!
3 People are very concerned about the _____ situation in this country.
4 Doctors recommend mothers to _____ their babies on their backs when they put them to bed.
5 You should be _____ of yourself for being so rude to my friends.
6 Being overweight can have serious long-term _____ on your health.
7 It's miserable weather, but I don't think you need an umbrella because it isn't _____ raining.
8 It's a formal dinner, so all the men will be wearing a _____ .
9 I wanted to go to the cinema and my girlfriend wanted to stay at home, but we finally reached a _____ and watched a DVD instead.
10 You can't _____ you've had one of my chocolates – there were three in the box and now there are only two!

6 LISTENING

a iChecker Listen to a radio programme about a book. In general, does the story have a sad or a happy ending?

b Listen again and mark the sentences T (true) or F (false).

1 Nazneen hadn't met Chanu before she joined him in England.
2 Nazneen's new husband doesn't live up to her expectations.
3 Nazneen rebels from the start against her new life in London.
4 Nazneen's feelings for her husband remain the same throughout the novel.
5 Nazneen's sister, Hasina, chose her own husband.
6 Nazneen doesn't make any friends while she is in London.
7 Nazneen's outlook on life changes as the novel progresses.
8 It is Nazneen's lover, Karim, who teaches her how to speak English.

c Listen again with the audio script on p.76 and try to guess the meaning of any words that you don't know. Then check in your dictionary.

The Joy Luck Club is the story of four Chinese mothers and their first-generation Chinese-American daughters; two generations of women struggling to come to terms with their cultural identity. Here Lindo Jong, one of the mothers, talks about her daughter, Waverley.

7 READING

a Read an extract from *The Joy Luck Club* by Amy Tan. Choose the sentence that best describes Lindo Jong's feelings about her daughter.

1 She is proud that her daughter can blend in with Chinese culture.

2 She regrets not being able to instil Chinese values in her daughter.

3 She is disappointed that her daughter does not take advantage of opportunities.

b Read the extract again and choose **a**, **b**, **c**, or **d**.

1 Lindo thinks her daughter will not be mistaken for a native-born Chinese mainly because of the way she… .
   a speaks   c smiles
   b looks   d dresses

2 Lindo's daughter… .
   a now wishes she had learnt to speak Chinese
   b never behaved like a Chinese person
   c has forgotten all the Chinese she ever knew
   d became less Chinese as she grew older

3 What Lindo most likes about the American way of life is that… .
   a you don't have to accept your fate
   b education is free for everyone
   c you can choose your religion
   d other people always help you

4 Which of these is *not* an aspect of Chinese character, according to Lindo?
   a hiding your real feelings
   b doing what your parents tell you to do
   c showing off
   d being aware of your strengths

5 Lindo gives the example of the chewing gum to show that… .
   a her daughter was stupid as a child
   b American habits were very easily acquired by her daughter
   c the American way of life is inferior to the Chinese
   d young people don't pay attention to adults

c Look at the highlighted verbs in the extract. What do you think they mean? Check in your dictionary.

LINDO JONG
Double Face

My daughter wanted to go to China for her second honeymoon, but now she is afraid.

'What if I blend in so well they think I'm one of them?' Waverley asked me. 'What if they don't let me come back to the United States?'

'When you go to China,' I told her, 'you don't even need to open your mouth. They already know you are an outsider.'

'What are you talking about?' she asked. My daughter likes to speak back. She likes to question what I say.

'Aii-ya,' I said. 'Even if you put on their clothes, even if you take off your makeup and hide your fancy jewelry, they know. They know just watching you walk, the way you carry your face. They know you do not belong.'

My daughter did not look pleased when I told her this, that she didn't look Chinese. She had a sour American look on her face. Oh, maybe ten years ago, she would have clapped her hands – hurray! – as if this were good news. But now she wants to be Chinese, it is so fashionable. And I know it is too late. All those years I tried to teach her! She followed my Chinese ways only until she learned to walk out the door by herself and go to school. So now the only Chinese words she can say are *sh-sh*, *houche*, *chr fan* and *gwan deng schweijyau*. How can she talk to people with those words only? Pee-pee, choo-choo train, eat, close light sleep. How can she think she can blend in? Only her skin and her hair are Chinese. Inside – she is all American-made.

It's my fault she is this way. I wanted my children to have the best combination: American circumstances and Chinese character. How could I know these two things do not mix?

I taught her how American circumstances work. If you are born poor here, it's no lasting shame. You are first in line for a scholarship. If the roof crashes on your head, no need to cry over this bad luck. You can sue anybody, make the landlord fix it. You do not have to sit like a Buddha under a tree letting pigeons drop their dirty business on your head. You can buy an umbrella. Or go inside a Catholic church. In America, nobody says you have to keep the circumstances somebody else gives you.

She learned these things, but I couldn't teach her about Chinese character. How to obey parents and listen to your mother's mind. How not to show your own thoughts, to put your feelings behind your face, so you can take advantage of hidden opportunities. Why easy things are not worth pursuing. How to know your own worth and polish it, never flashing it around like a cheap ring. Why Chinese thinking is best.

No, this kind of thinking didn't stick to her. She was too busy chewing gum, blowing bubbles bigger than her cheeks. Only that kind of thinking stuck.

'Finish your coffee,' I told her yesterday. 'Don't throw your blessings away.'

'Don't be so old-fashioned,' she told me, finishing her coffee down the sink. 'I'm my own person.'

And I think, How can she be her own person? When did I give her up?

> Whenever I feel the need to exercise,
> I lie down until it goes away.
>
> *Paul Terry, American animator*

10B A good sport

1 LEXIS IN CONTEXT
Battle of the workouts

Look at the Lexis in Context on Student's Book p.99. Then complete the words connected with the body and exercise.

1 The swimmer filled her l*ungs* with air before she dived into the pool.
2 I've started doing s_____-u_____ every morning to strengthen my stomach muscles.
3 Cyclists usually have very muscular th_____.
4 Some experts now say that just three minutes of v_____ exercise a week is enough to improve your fitness.
5 She went to see a doctor about a chronic pain in the lower area of her sp_____.
6 My brother is in tr_____ to participate in next year's London Marathon.
7 After taking up yoga, she noticed she had more fl_____ in her joints.
8 The trainer makes the players do ten pr_____-u_____ if they miss football practice.
9 You should warm up and st_____ your muscles before playing sport.
10 Many people focus on their arms and legs in the gym, but I try to strengthen my tr_____ as well.

2 VOCABULARY
word building: adjectives, nouns, and verbs

Complete the sentences with the correct form of the words in brackets.

1 She added some flour to _thicken_ the sauce. (thick)
2 My son is now the same _____ as me! (high)
3 The builders need to _____ the ground before they can build the new car park. (flat)
4 The sleeves of my new jacket are too long. Can you _____ them for me? (short)
5 My grandmother can't walk very far – she has no _____ in her legs. (strong)
6 Check the _____ before diving in. (deep)
7 Working so hard for so long _____ his health and finally he fell ill. (weak)
8 This mascara promises to _____ your eyelashes, but I'm not sure I believe it. (long)
9 We measured the _____ of the space before buying a new cupboard. (wide)

3 GRAMMAR relative clauses

a (Circle) the correct answers. One, two, or three of the answers may be correct. (— = no relative pronoun)

1 The referee showed a red card to the players (that) / (who) / — had been fighting.
2 This is the room *that | where | which* the players get changed.
3 He only scored two goals last season, both *that | of which | which* were penalties.
4 She's the model *which | who | whose* husband plays basketball for the NBA.
5 The surface *where | which | —* Spanish tennis players like best is clay.
6 We lost the final 3-2, *that | which | —* was a shame.
7 That's the match *that | which | —* I saw live at their stadium.
8 Our coach doesn't know *that | what | which* is wrong with our best player.
9 My sister, *that | who | —* once played hockey for England, has recently qualified as a P.E. teacher.
10 The woman *who | whom | to whom* he dedicated the goal is his new girlfriend.

b Join the sentences using a relative pronoun if necessary and the right punctuation if it is a non-defining relative clause.

1 A friend gave us the tickets. He couldn't go to the match.
The friend _who gave us the tickets couldn't go to the match_ .
2 My cousin is a cross-country runner. He has been given a scholarship by an American university.
My cousin _____ .
3 There's been a frost. This means that the match will probably be cancelled.
There _____ .
4 Our team has two goalkeepers. Neither of them can play next weekend.
Our team _____ .
5 I've only had these trainers for a week. They've broken already.
These trainers _____ .
6 We spoke to a steward. He directed us to our seats.
We _____ .
7 I bought a new racket for my son. It wasn't very expensive.
The racket _____ .
8 The showers are very rarely cleaned. Many of them do not work properly.
The showers _____ .

4 PRONUNCIATION homographs

a Match the phonetics to the sentences.

1 b /kən'tent/
   a /'kɒntent/

   a The problem with your essay is not the style,
      but the content.
   b The problem with my parents is that they're
      never content with anything I do.

2 ☐ /juːs/
   ☐ /juːz/

   a They've prohibited the use of chemical weapons.
   b They use uranium to produce nuclear energy.

3 ☐ /kləʊz/
   ☐ /kləʊs/

   a Can you close the window, please? I'm cold.
   b Can you move up? You're sitting too close to me.

4 ☐ /teə/
   ☐ /tɪə/

   a I cried in pain and wiped away a tear.
   b I would never tear a page out of a library book.

5 ☐ /maɪ'njuːt/
   ☐ /'mɪnɪt/

   a I'm still hungry. That restaurant serves minute
      portions of food.
   b Let's wait outside. The restaurant will be open
      in a minute.

6 ☐ /raʊ/
   ☐ /rəʊ/

   a We're not speaking because we've had a row.
   b We sat in the back row so we couldn't be seen.

7 ☐ /waʊnd/
   ☐ /wuːnd/

   a She cleaned his wound and put on a plaster.
   b She wound the string into a ball to use it later.

b **iChecker** Listen and check. Practise saying
   the sentences.

5 LISTENING

a **iChecker** Listen to a radio programme about
   children and sport. Which sport are the children
   learning and how competitive is it?

b Listen again and complete the notes.

> Joseph Ting and Luke Walden are the [1]_____ of
> a children's sports club called Rugby Munchkins. The
> youngest members are only [2]_____ years old.
> The club is open to [3]_____. Classes are held on
> Saturday and [4]_____ and are ideal for children who
> enjoy doing [5]_____ activities. Coaches teach the
> sport by playing [6]_____ with the children. One of
> these is called Hungry Munchkins, and the aim is for the
> children in [7]_____ teams to collect the balls which
> belong to their team. Older children sometimes play
> a match, and after the final whistle, they are all given a
> [8]_____ as a reward.

c Listen again with the audio script on p.76 and try to
   guess the meaning of any words that you don't know.
   Then check in your dictionary.

6 READING

a Read the article once. According to Michael Mosley, which of the following is most likely to keep a person healthy?

1 Going on a strict diet.

2 Short periods of exercise.

3 Cycling for an hour.

4 Going to the gym.

b Six sentences and paragraphs have been removed from the article. Read it again and match A–G to the gaps 1–6. There is one sentence or paragraph you do not need to use.

A So that's the problem with exercising at the gym. You walk briskly on the treadmill for 30 minutes (200 calories). You then have a congratulatory muffin. You've burnt 200 calories and consumed 500. It doesn't compute.

B I'm still unconvinced that a mere three minutes' vigorous exercise a week can control our fitness, predict our future health and prevent common diseases, but Mosley has no doubts.

C So, if diets tend not to work, what about exercise? Surely regular visits to a gym – 20 minutes on the bike or running machine, two or three times a week – will do the trick?

D The 54-year-old graduated in Philosophy, Politics and Economics from Oxford University and spent a couple of years in banking, following, one assumes, in the footsteps of his banker father. He, though, changed direction.

E I order tea for both of us first and then begin my questioning. I start by asking Mosley to what extent a change in eating habits can improve one's health.

F Mosley explains that he keeps moving by getting up and walking around every hour when he's working at his desk. He cycles a mile and a half to the station every day, building a minute of HIT into his trip, and takes the stairs instead of the lift.

G 'Scientists are looking at what's required for good health. And it's inactivity that causes the problems of fat around the organs and the metabolic problems that lead to diabetes. The average person sits for 12 to 14 hours a day.'

c Look at the highlighted words and phrases. What do you think they mean? Check in your dictionary.

The truth about exercise?

I am comfortably seated by the fire in the tearoom of Brown's Hotel in London when a bundle of energy comes to a halt at my side. Enter Michael Mosley, the BBC's most valuable communicator of complex scientific ideas. We're here to discuss his latest theory: that three minutes of vigorous exercise a week is enough to keep you healthy; and that, generally speaking, exercise contributes very little to weight loss.

1 _____ He launches into an explanation of why diets generally fail. 'It's not that people are weak-willed. It's pretty easy to lose weight quickly on a strict diet, but then the body conspires against you. Fear of starvation is a basic instinct. As you lose weight your metabolic rate slows. Your body encourages you to conserve calories by moving less. The brain tells the nerve cells in your intestine that you're hungry. Thus, 95 per cent of diets fail.'

2 _____ 'Not so. We grossly underestimate the amount of time you need to burn calories. If you cycle steadily for an hour you'll burn 500 calories. That's one muffin. You'd have to cycle from Nottingham to Leeds – 78 miles – to burn a pound of fat, and one experiment in the USA showed that even thinking about exercise triggers the hormonal response that makes you want to eat.'

3 _____ Putting weight loss aside, can just three minutes of exercise a week really be as useful as three hours on the treadmill? The answer lies, it seems, in the acronym HIT. It stands for High-Intensity Interval Training, and research suggests that this short-burst approach is highly effective.

4 _____ 'But if we move around, we activate a protein which takes fat out of the bloodstream and transfers it to the muscles, where it can be burnt.'

5 _____ 'What studies are showing is that keeping active is the answer to many problems,' he says. The HIT approach, combined with gentler exercise such as walking from room to room, will do the trick.

6 _____ Mosley isn't at all worried about the damaging impact this research could have on the gym and dieting industries. He heads off to the station at a smart pace. I pay the bill and catch a cab. Must do better!

Listening

1 A))

Speaker 1 Speaking from my own personal situation, I love the fact that I have a brother. Um, it provided, he provided me with a lot of fun when, when we were growing up um, and um and having, having two kids myself I am very pleased that they, they've got each other to look after. And, er, I think as you go through life and your own parents get older, um and you know, you will one day have to look after them, I think doing that with a, with a sibling would be a lot easier.

Speaker 2 I'm an only child, and someone said to me, 'Oh that must be so much better to be an only child because you get all your parents' attention and you don't have to share it with your brothers and sisters,' and to an extent I kind of agree because um, you, it is wonderful to have all that attention from your parents. But, you can end up becoming, sort of spoilt and um used to having this attention, so when you have to go to school or you have to interact with other people, if you don't get the attention that you've been used to, you can react in a, in a really spoilt way without, sort of, meaning to.

Speaker 3 I've got two children and although they fight all the time and they, you know, all this sort of thing, there's, I think, I often, well when they are fighting, try and look at the positives of it and think, well, I suppose it's a good thing that they are sort of, you know, learning to do all those things within a safe family environment, which I suppose if you are, I mean, if you are an only child, perhaps then it has to be at school or, you know, it's like practising.

Speaker 4 I'd hate to have been an only child, I mean I had three brothers and sisters, and I think only, there was, the girl next door was an only child and she was under so much pressure from her parents to succeed and all their hopes were focused on this one girl ... I thought, I wouldn't want all that pressure on me.

1 B))

1 Well, one job I've always rather fancied is being a travel writer, I mean, basically because I like travelling and I like going round the world and I'd like to have an excuse to do it and someone to pay me to do it if possible, um, and I think I would be quite good at it because, well, I am quite sociable and I like to think I can write and er, and I'm quite good at living out of a suitcase and living cheap, um and it just seems to be a wonderful way of seeing the world. I mean, I don't actually know anybody who does it, but I've always sort of envied people like Michael Palin who do these television series going all round the world and they seem to have such a wonderful time.

But I have occasionally had to read travel books and some of them are brilliant and some you definitely get the impression that they've been sent there by their publisher to do a travel book about Patagonia or whatever it is and nothing much has happened, but they've still got to write the book. So you get rather a boring drudgy book sometimes, and I suppose that might be a drawback that you'd feel you had to write a book even if you'd got nothing to say.

2 Well, what I'd really hate to do is any sort of job on a production line, any sort of real drudgery where there's really no, sort of, mental input at all, but you're just repeating the same task again and again and again and I think that would probably drive me insane.

I have done something a bit like it when I was about 18, I worked in a plastics factory to earn some money for a couple of months and I remember I went in, in the dark and I came out in the dark, because it was winter, so I never saw the light of day, it was about a ten-hour day, paid almost nothing, we had half an hour for lunch and the noise of the machines was so loud that you could, you could shout at the top of your voice and the person next to you couldn't hear you, and the smell of plastics filled the air and it was absolutely hideous. The only, the only advantage was that it was so loud that you could actually sing at the top of your voice and nobody could hear, so I spent a lot of my day singing to myself, which, which I quite enjoyed.

2 A))

Interviewer Do you find it easier to understand native or non-native speakers of English?

Zoltan It depends what you mean. As far as pronunciation goes, it's a lot easier to understand native speakers with a standard accent like BBC English or General American. And for me, some of the regional dialects are quite easy to understand as well. Um, other dialects are a lot harder to decipher, like Scots, or Geordie, or New Zealand are really hard to understand. As far as content is concerned, it's a lot easier to understand non-native speakers. Because they don't use idiomatic expressions or obscure cultural references; they don't use regional slang. They also use the Latin, er, verb instead of a phrasal verb, for example like 'continue' rather than 'carry on', which is less easy to confuse. And the other thing about non-native speakers is that they are a lot more direct. When they speak in English, they say what they mean. There are no... allusions and metaphors and references to other things.

Interviewer How do you feel about having your English corrected?

Zoltan I don't mind. Er, I'm sometimes annoyed with myself for making a recurring mistake again like mixing up 'he' and 'she' and I find it a bit weird when a non-native speaker who is less fluent than me corrects my English. And ... I also think that non-native speakers, good non-native speakers, are often better at spelling than native speakers, because we learn words with their spelling whereas native speakers learn the word first and learn the spelling years later. And just recently an English friend of mine corrected my spelling of 'accommodation', which I'd spelt with double 'c' and double 'm', and he insisted that it was spelled with a single 'm' and in fact I was right.

Interviewer Do you have any funny or embarrassing stories related to misunderstanding someone?

Zoltan Hungarians aren't generally interested in bird watching, and most Hungarians I know can't tell one bird from another. And recently a friend of mine told me about seeing some kites over, over the fields near their house the previous weekend. And I said that flying kites is really popular in Budapest too, meaning that people go in to the hills at the weekend to fly their home-made paper kites. It never occurred to me for a second that she may be talking about a bird. I don't think a Hungarian would ever tell someone else about seeing some bird several days before.

Interviewer Is there anything you still find difficult about English?

Zoltan Not really. I've been learning English for 26 years. If I had to say anything, I would say counting, numbers. If I have to count anything, I have to switch back to Hungarian, even if the person I'm speaking to will need the English sum.

Interviewer Do you find it easier to understand native or non-native speakers of English?

Cristina Well, it all depends where they come from. I suppose it's more or less the same. Some non-natives are more difficult than others if you're not used to the accent. For instance, I used to find some Japanese and Chinese speakers difficult to understand, but then because of work I went to the Far East lots of times and then it became OK. Natives, again it all depends. I was taught RP and one assumes that everybody speaks that, and of course I had friends from lots of parts of Britain who did not speak RP. In fact, it is a pretty rare thing these days. So we have a good friend from, from Glasgow and it was always embarrassing for me because I could not understand most of what he was saying. I still don't.

Interviewer How do you feel about having your English corrected?

Cristina I don't mind. My children used to love correcting me. They still say I speak very funny English, but usually adults in this country do not correct you. I would like to be corrected.

Interviewer Do you have any funny or embarrassing stories related to misunderstanding someone?

Cristina Um yes, misunderstanding and being misunderstood. Several! Some I don't think I would like to tell you about, but I'll tell you one. I was a student at the University of Michigan in the United States and my phonetics professor was very handsome and therefore I did extremely well, not in all subjects, but it was worth studying that one. But I remember my first tutorial when he said 'See you later' and I thought, 'Hmm, interesting. Where?' And in class he'd said, I'd asked a question and

he'd said, 'Interesting question' so I thought, 'Great! He thinks I'm clever, and maybe he thinks I'm interesting to meet somewhere else, but I couldn't understand how I was going to find out where or when. I luckily didn't ask. It would have been very embarrassing.

Interviewer Is there anything you still find difficult about English?

Cristina Yes, I think there are things that have especially to do with cultural aspects. I used to find when my children were little that I didn't know the same nursery rhymes that you know here. I didn't know the actions, and I still don't know lots of things. It's, I don't know to give an example, say I had learnt American English, but I still didn't know who the Simpsons were.

2 B))

Speaker 1 My earliest memory is from when I was about three years old and I was at home with my mum and I was playing with my red plastic hoover, which I really liked as a toy when I was little. Um, it might have seemed a bit dull but I really enjoyed playing with it.

Speaker 2 My earliest memory is of, er, living in Malta when I was young and looking out of the window to see, um, the grapevine and the veranda outside my bedroom window having been destroyed by a whirlwind that had just gone through the, gone through the garden of the house. It hadn't touched the house itself just taken out the veranda and the grapevine.

Speaker 3 My earliest memory is my first day of school when I was about five because I was really nervous and I forgot to tell the other people my name so people were kind of confused.

Speaker 4 My earliest memory is probably at the local airport, but um I've got a feeling that it's a memory of looking at a photograph of myself in a basket at the local airport. So it's a bit hard to distinguish whether that's a real memory or a perceived one.

Speaker 5 Um, my earliest memory is walking on a beach with my family collecting shells. I somehow remember finding a piece of blue glass which had been worn smooth by the waves. When I showed it to my mum, she told me to keep it because it was such a pretty colour.

3 A))

Speaker 1 My best friend kept insisting that I met up with a cute, single male friend of hers. Finally, I gave in and went on a date. My friend was right: he really was cute and single. But he was totally obsessed with my friend – all he did was talk about her. I finally made an excuse to go home early after he asked me if I thought my friend was happy with her boyfriend!

Speaker 2 I was on my first date with this beautiful young lady, and we went to a nice restaurant. The waitress was bringing our drinks to us when one of the other waitresses asked her a question. And as she turned around, she tipped our drinks all over me – I mean, I was drenched from head to toe. Other than that, though, the date went really well. We got married after six months and well, now, fifteen years later, we still laugh about our first date.

Speaker 3 This is one of my more memorable dates, but for quite the wrong reason. What we did was this: he took me for a loooooong drive in his truck – I had absolutely no idea where we were. Then he stopped at a gas station and bought me an ice cream. And then he drove me back home again. That was it. As you can imagine, I didn't bother to find out what would happen the second time round.

Speaker 4 My most memorable first date was at a fast food restaurant! I'd been trying to get together with this girl for weeks, but our schedules just didn't coincide. So, when I was going out for a burger one evening, I just texted her and asked her to come. And amazingly, she did! And we ended up talking about everything from work to family. We've been together for eight months now, and she often pulls my leg about it.

Speaker 5 When my current boyfriend asked me out, we went out for dinner and then back to my place for coffee. And at some point he got down on his knees, you know, like he was going to propose, or something – and he got me really worried. Then he got a ring pull out of his pocket – you know, the ones that come off the top of a drinks can – and he said, 'Will you be my girlfriend?' And after that, we couldn't stop laughing.

3 B)))

Speaker 1 Erm, as far as historical films go, my personal favourite is *Elizabeth*. Um, as the title suggests, it's about one of the most famous queens of England, Elizabeth I, who ruled the country in the second half of the sixteenth century. The plot is based on the early years of her reign, when she is on the lookout for a suitable husband. Cate Blanchett plays the role of Elizabeth, and she looks wonderful in the flowing gowns typical of that era. In fact, all the actors look the part, because of the great attention paid to what each of the characters is wearing.

Speaker 2 I think my favourite historical film is Ben Affleck's thriller *Argo*. The film tells the story of the rescue of six American diplomats in Iran when relations between the two countries were starting to break down in the late 1970s. Erm, it's got to be one of the most exciting films I've ever seen – I spent the whole time sitting on the edge of my seat. Some of the events may be a bit exaggerated, but it's a true story all the same.

Speaker 3 Erm, my favourite historical film has got to be *The Last Emperor*. It's based on the autobiography of the last emperor of China, Puyi, who died in 1967. Puyi grew up in the Forbidden City in Beijing, and the film's director, Bernardo Bertolucci, was lucky enough – he got permission to film inside this amazing palace in Beijing. I mean, visually, the film is absolutely stunning, so it's not surprising that it won nine Oscars.

Speaker 4 Erm, I thoroughly enjoyed the historical film *Invictus* when it came out. Um, it's about the events that occurred in South Africa before and during the Rugby World Cup in 1995, I think. And there are two great actors in it: Morgan Freeman, he plays Nelson Mandela, the President of South Africa at the time, and Matt Damon. He plays the captain of the rugby team. They're both brilliant in the parts. I like it because at first they're hostile to each other and then they become friends. That's why I like the film.

Speaker 5 This film isn't particularly well-known, er, but it's definitely my favourite historical film. It's a drama called *Agora*, and it's based on the life of a Greek philosopher called Hypatia, who lived in Roman Egypt in the fourth century. Hypatia was also a mathematician and an astronomer and she taught at a school in Alexandria. Hypatia is admired by many, including myself, for giving her life trying to protect the library of Alexandria when it was attacked.

4 A)))

Our composer of the week this week is Aberdeen-born percussionist, Dame Evelyn Glennie. She studied at the Royal Academy of Music. In a career spanning more than 20 years, she has performed with almost all of the world's leading orchestras, playing up to 60 different percussion instruments, from the xylophone to the timpani. In that time, she has won over 80 international music awards, including two Grammies. Outside classical music, she has achieved crossover success in the worlds of pop and rock, having recorded with artists such as Sting and Björk as well as composing and performing a number of soundtracks for film and television.

Glennie began studying music at the age of 12, by which time she was profoundly deaf. However, she has never been deterred by her loss of hearing and doesn't see it as an obstacle to composing and performing music. In fact, she is frustrated by the fact that despite all her achievements as a musician, it's her deafness that always makes the headlines. As she writes on her website in her essay about hearing, 'If you are standing by the road and a large truck goes by you, do you hear or feel the vibration? The answer is both. For some reason we tend to make a distinction between hearing a sound and feeling a vibration, in reality they are the same thing.' She goes on to point out that this distinction doesn't exist in all languages. For example, in Italian, the verb 'sentire' means 'to hear' while the same verb in the reflexive form means 'to feel'.

In concert and in the studio, Glennie performs barefoot in order to feel the sounds of her instruments vibrating through the floor, and the title of her best-selling autobiography is *Good Vibrations*. But let's get on to the music. Glennie released her first album in…

4 B)))

Presenter If you're a regular cinema-goer, you may have noticed the long list of films that have been shown recently which are based on books. Yet it can't be easy to turn literature into cinema successfully. Today, we're going to take a look at the subject of film adaptations and we've invited film buff Lindsey Wallace into the studio to share her views with us. Hello, Lindsey.

Lindsey Hi there.

Presenter Lindsey, what is it that makes a good film adaptation?

Lindsey Basically, it's finding the right balance between telling the original story while at the same time adding something new to it. If there are too many changes to the plot, the fans will get upset, but if the film is too faithful to the original, they'll go away wondering why they bothered to see it in the first place.

Presenter Are you suggesting that the film adaptation doesn't have to be 100% faithful to the book?

Lindsey It isn't really a question of being faithful to the book; it's more a question of capturing the spirit of the original story. A good screenplay writer is one who understands the material and is able to pick out the themes, characters and scenes that are most important. After that, it's a question of timing – deciding how much or how little emphasis to place on each of these things.

Presenter Hmm. Apart from the balance and the timing, is there anything else that contributes to a good film adaptation?

Lindsey Well, once you've got the screenplay right, you obviously have to find the right actors for all the different roles. Casting is fundamental when it comes to film adaptations, as readers will already have an idea in their minds of what the characters are like.

Presenter Lindsey, now that we've established what makes a good film adaptation, can you give us an example?

Lindsey Um, actually, I can give you more: the three films that make up *The Lord of the Rings* series. All of them have an exceptional cast including renowned actors such as Elijah Wood, Ian McKellen, Liv Tyler, and Cate Blanchett. And the makers have been faithful to the J.R.R. Tolkien novels; at times parts of the original narrative are read over the images that appear on the screen. At the same time, the timing is impeccable as the film focuses on what is truly important in the story. But the key to the film's success is Peter Jackson's use of special effects, some of which had never been seen in the cinema before.

Presenter What kind of special effects?

Lindsey Take, for example, the character of Gollum, a creature created almost entirely by computer-generated images. You believe he's really there next to the real actors on the screen.

Presenter That's very true. How about giving us an example of a bad film adaptation, Lindsey?

Lindsey Again, I'm going to give you another film series: *The Hunger Games*. The films are hugely popular and have won several different awards. I think the casting is certainly excellent, and

Jennifer Lawrence is superb as the central character, Katniss Everdeen. But I feel that the filmmakers have been a bit too faithful to the books. Each film tells the story in the exact order that it happens in the original, which, to me, makes the plot seem a bit flat. There is little use of timing, so the key scenes aren't given enough emphasis. On top of this, I don't think there's really anything new for the readers – even the colour and flamboyance of the Capitol comes as no surprise as it is depicted just as it is in the book, which I found a bit disappointing.

Presenter That's a shame because all three of the books were excellent. Lindsey Wallace, thank you for joining us today.

Lindsey My pleasure.

5 A))

Presenter Time flies, as the saying goes, and it's quite true. Gone are the lazy days of childhood when the summer holidays seemed to crawl by – once you become an adult, the weeks pass by in a whirl of activity. An American neuroscientist has recently published a paper exploring this phenomenon. Our science expert, Stephen, is here with us to explain the theory. Stephen, why does time seem to go so slowly when we're children and so fast when we grow up?

Stephen First of all, it's important to understand how we perceive time. Essentially, our brains take in a whole lot of information from our senses and organize it in a way that makes sense to us before we ever perceive it. When we receive lots of new information, it takes our brains a while to process it all. The longer this processing takes, the longer that period of time feels. Conversely, if your brain doesn't have to process lots of new information, time seems to go much faster.

Presenter Well how does that explain why our perception of time changes as we get older?

Stephen When we're younger, most of the information we receive is brand new – and there's lots of it. The new information takes longer to process, which is why time seems to pass more slowly. Whereas when we are older, the world is much more familiar to us, so there is less new information to process. It doesn't take long to process anything that's new, which explains why time seems to pass more quickly.

Presenter Uh-uh. Stephen, is there anything we can do to slow time down?

Stephen The good news is that there is, yes. The first thing you can do is to keep learning. If you're constantly reading, trying new activities or taking courses to learn new skills, you'll be feeding your brain with loads of new information that will make time pass more slowly.

Presenter Hmm. That sounds easy. What else?

Stephen The second thing you can do is to visit new places. A new environment can send a mass of information rushing to your brain: smells, sounds, people, colours, textures. Your brain has to interpret all of this, which will give it plenty of work to do.

Presenter I suppose meeting new people might help as well?

Stephen That's right. Meeting new people is a good workout for our brains because it takes a lot of time and effort to process and understand details about them.

Presenter Hmm. Is there anything else we can do, Stephen?

Stephen Yes, being spontaneous can help a lot. Surprises are like new activities: they make us pay attention and heighten our senses.

Presenter Well, so, now you know. All you have to do if you want to slow down time is to follow Stephen's advice. Stephen Carter, thank you for joining us.

Stephen My pleasure.

5 B))

Presenter Hello and welcome to the show. Today we're looking at different ways of saving money, and we're asking you, the listeners, to phone in with any ideas you've experimented with. The number you need to call is 081 272 272 and the lines are already open. And it looks as if we have a caller on line 1. Can you tell us your name, please?

Caller 1 Yes, I'm Mary.

Presenter Hello, Mary. What's your money-saving idea, please?

Caller 1 Well, when I noticed that my energy bill kept creeping up and up, I decided to turn down the thermostat on my heating. Instead of having it at 21°, I've put it down to 18°, and it's made a big difference. I pay about fifty pounds less on my heating bill than I did before, and if I feel a bit cold, I put an extra jumper on.

Presenter That sounds like a great idea, Mary. Most of us have our heating on too high, so it makes sense to turn it down to pay less – and save energy at the same time. OK, thanks Mary. There's another caller on line 2 – Philip, is that right?

Caller 2 Yes, it is.

Presenter What do you do to save money, Philip?

Caller 2 Um, I always take a packed lunch to work. We've got a small kitchen on my floor with a microwave, so we can bring our food in a plastic box and heat it up. I usually take what's left from dinner the night before, but if there isn't anything hot, I make a salad. It's certainly a lot cheaper than having to pay for a meal every day.

Presenter Thanks for that, Philip. Yeah, taking a packed lunch is an excellent way of saving money when you need to have lunch at work. OK, our next caller is Emily. How do you try to save money, Emily?

Caller 3 Um, yes, um, a couple of years ago, I decided to start putting all my change in a coin jar at the end of the day. I've got one of those big sweet jars, so it takes quite a long time to fill it up. It's my way of saving up to go away in the summer – I wouldn't be able to afford it, otherwise.

Presenter Those sweet jars are great for saving money in, aren't they, Emily? OK, back to line 2 for our next caller. What's your name, please?

Caller 4 Jonathan.

Presenter Jonathan, tell us your money-saving idea.

Caller 4 Well, it might sound a bit radical, but I cut up all of my credit cards last year. Now, I only use cash. Paying in cash really makes you think about how much you're spending – if you use a credit card, you tend to lose control, to some extent. It's worked for me, anyway, and I've cut my spending by about 20%.

Presenter Jonathan, that's certainly the bravest solution we've had so far. OK, we've just got time for one more call, Wendy on line 1. What's your money-saving idea?

Caller 5 Um, it might sound a bit weird, but I've found that it's a really bad idea to go shopping on an empty stomach. When I'm hungry, I end up buying loads of snacks on impulse – it's such a waste of money. So now I do my shopping straight after I've had a meal and I don't spend half as much.

Presenter That makes sense, Wendy, thank you for calling. Well, I hope that the rest of our listeners have found those ideas useful. And now it's time for the news…

I found Matt Cutts' TED talk extremely encouraging, so much so that it motivated me to think up some activities for you all to try. Here are just a few of them.

Summer is just around the corner, so let's start with things you can do outside. First of all, there's running. There's an app you can get that helps you build up to running five kilometres. It only takes half an hour of your day, three days a week, so make the most of those longer days, get out of the office or gym, and try a run in the park.

If you don't fancy running, you could try walking to work for a month. If that isn't possible, you could walk to public transport or get up early every day and walk around the block. Walking is a great way to start the day and you'll soon discover that fresh air is your friend.

Apart from physical activity, summer is a great time to look at what you eat. Why not have a go at making a new salad every day? It's possible to make at least 30 different salads, and there are some marvellous recipes out there. This challenge has the added bonus of being a health kick as well.

So much for the summer months; what about when it starts to cool off and you have to stay indoors? One thing you could do is start a book club. When I last moved house, I left a brilliant book club behind and immediately missed the witty and jovial conversations I used to have with the other members. So I started a book club of my own in my new neighbourhood. If you love reading, and you're not in a book club, get it sorted immediately.

If you prefer writing to reading, you could start your own blog. Pick something you're really passionate about and start blogging about it. It's fun, free, and takes up hours of your time – literally, hours.

Another activity for the winter months is to learn a new language. There's another app that provides a fun, game-like way to learn languages such as French, German, Italian, Spanish, Portuguese, Dutch, Turkish, Hungarian, Polish, or Romanian – for free.

These are just a few ideas for you to try, but the possibilities are endless. All you need to do is pick an activity and get started. I'm sure you won't regret it!

Speaker 1 What's the question? Do I have any obsessions? Well, I don't consider them obsessions, but I do have a habit of organizing myself in ways that other people might consider obsessive. I've walked into a friend's flat where I was staying for a week or two, and instantly alphabetized their collection of CDs or DVDs of maybe a hundred or so because if I was going to be there, and I needed to find a piece of music, it just means… it was a lot easier to find it when it's alphabetized.

Speaker 2 Yeah, this started sometime last year. I was surfing to discover something about my youngest child's skin problem, when I found this amazing parenting website. Soon I found I couldn't go a day without logging on. Um, I started spending all evening 'chatting' to my new online friends instead of spending time with my kids and my husband. It never crossed my mind that it could be addictive, but now I feel edgy and tense if I can't access my computer.

Speaker 3 Well, I do. I've got a complete obsession about cleaning, and it's awful, it's the bane of my life, it's absolutely awful, I cannot relax unless everything is absolutely, you know, um, clean and tidy. I've had to let it go a bit because my husband's an Aussie and he's very laid-back and I just haven't been allowed to be as obsessed as I have been in the past, and of course having children stops the obsession a little bit because there's toys and stuff everywhere…

Speaker 4 My addiction has got me into a lot of trouble, actually. I've always loved spending money, and I guess I never realized that it could get out of hand. Coming home with armfuls of clothes gave me an enormous high and I needed to keep on buying more clothes, shoes, and accessories to keep getting it. I would go in my lunch hour, after work and at weekends, but I couldn't see that I had a problem until my boyfriend, James, split up with me. On top of that, I'm about £30,000 in debt now.

Speaker 5 There's a name for this condition, but I can't remember what it is and I'm not sure what it's called but I do count things. If I come into a room, I will count the number of lights on the ceiling. The only thing is, I don't know how many there really are, because I count things so that they turn out to be in multiples of threes or nines, and I also count panes in windows, I will count panels in doors. But I like them always to get up to a 3 or a 30 or a 90, um, so it's a fairly useless thing, but it's just something I just do.

Interviewer Anna, the school you attended was quite different from a conventional school, wasn't it?

Anna Yes, it was. I went to a Steiner School.

Interviewer Hmm. Can you briefly explain to us what that is?

Anna Yes, it's a school that follows the theory of Rudolf Steiner, an Austrian philosopher. The idea is that school should help a child develop the tools to be able to learn what he or she wants to rather than having knowledge delivered to them. Steiner schools have been around for about a hundred years now.

Interviewer Hmm, very interesting. Now, how long were you at the Steiner School, Anna?

Anna I did the lot there – from four to 18. I went all the way from kindergarten to 'A' levels. I got an 'A' level in art – um, you know, the Steiner system is heavily focused on creativity and the arts. In general, the question of exams is a bit of a grey area in Steiner Schools, because, well, they don't really fit into the whole philosophy of it at all.

Interviewer Yes, I'd heard that. Um, where exactly was the school you went to, Anna?

Anna Er, it was about 15 miles from my house. My dad used to take us there in his big, red delivery van. There were about ten of us and he would drive round picking everybody up. This was in the days before health and safety; none of us wore seatbelts. In fact, there weren't any seats in the back of the van, so everybody just piled in and sat on the floor. Oh, the school run was a lot of fun – we had a party every morning.

Interviewer Yes. What about when you got to school?

Anna Um, kindergarten was great. All the toys were made of natural materials; we had lots of lovely wooden toys. And we did lots of fun activities like singing and baking. But that doesn't mean that we were left to wander around freely. It's, it's quite a structured approach, and everything is done for a reason.

Interviewer What about after kindergarten – what were the classes like then?

Anna Um, the ones I remember most are the art classes, because I loved them. Um, by art, I don't just mean painting and drawing. We did things like woodwork and metalwork and lots of crafty stuff like sewing and, er, weaving. No other school would have offered me the same opportunities as I had there, and it totally set me up to do what I do now.

Interviewer Which is...?

Anna I design and make furniture – it's all very hands-on. At university I studied ceramics: I did a BA in Cardiff and then an MA at the Royal College of Art, London. I use a lot of ceramics in my work, making ceramic lighting and that kind of thing. Actually, all of my peer group ended up doing something creative with their lives: some went into music and acting. That's the kind of thing a Steiner education prepares you for.

Interviewer Hmm. Anna, you have children of your own now. Are you planning on sending them to a Steiner School?

Anna Er...probably not, no, although it very much depends on them. The twins are only two months old, so I still don't know how their personalities will develop. If I see that one of them is artistic, or that one would benefit from smaller classes, then I might consider it, but in general, I'd rather my kids grew up in the real world.

Interviewer It sounds as if you have some regrets about your education, Anna.

Anna I'm not sure 'regrets' would be the right word, because a Steiner education wasn't the wrong thing for me. I loved it until I was about 12, when I began to realize that I was living in a kind of bubble and I started to rebel against that. I also wish I could have had more of an academic input in the later years – that would have opened a lot more doors for me.

Interviewer Anna, it's been really interesting talking to you. Thank you so much for your time.

Anna No problem.

7 B))

Presenter Hello and welcome to today's programme where we're looking at the works of Russian-born artist Vladimir Tretchikoff. Now, Tretchikoff's most famous painting *The Chinese Girl* was recently sold for almost £1 million at auction in London. Our art expert is in the studio with us to tell us about the woman who modelled for the picture, Monika Pon-su-san. Louise, was Monika a professional model?

Louise No, not at all. She was a young Chinese girl, working in her uncle's laundry in Cape Town, South Africa. She was only 17 at the time, and when she met Tretchikoff, she had never modelled before.

Presenter How did the two meet?

Louise Tretchikoff had heard of Monika's beauty from a friend, and so he went to the laundry to see her himself. According to Monika, she was serving a customer when he came in, and while he was waiting he couldn't take his eyes off of her. Once they were alone, he introduced himself and asked if he could paint her.

Presenter That must have come as a surprise to Monika. Did she actually know who he was?

Louise Yes, she did, in fact. By chance, she had read about him in a newspaper the Saturday before, so she knew who he was.

Presenter Louise, let's talk about the painting itself. Is Monika wearing her own clothes?

Louise No. Apparently, Tretchikoff gave her one of his wife's silk gowns to put on. But the real gown wasn't yellow like the one in the painting; it was blue.

Presenter What about Monika's expression in the picture? Why is she looking so serious?

Louise Monika says that as Tretchikoff was painting her, she was thinking about the traumas he had experienced in his life. He was imprisoned several times during the war, and at one point he lost contact with his wife and his daughter.

Presenter Hmm. But the story has a happy ending, doesn't it, because his family was reunited in Cape Town.

Louise That's right. It was fortunate that they all ended up in the same place.

Presenter Louise, did Tretchikoff pay Monika for modelling for him?

Louise Yes, he did. He gave her just over six South African pounds. That's the equivalent of around 130 pounds today.

Presenter That doesn't seem much. Did she at least like the painting?

Louise No, she was shocked by the green face. She says she thought that she looked like a monster. And she didn't think much of the title, either: *The Chinese Girl*. She was expecting something a little more exotic.

Presenter And what happened to her afterwards? Did she ever model again?

Louise No, she never posed for another painting. She got married and went to Johannesburg, where she had five children before splitting up with her husband. After that, she had to go back to work to try and make ends meet, but the family never had much money.

Presenter In contrast to Tretchikoff, who went on to make a fortune. Louise, did Monika manage to attend the auction of the painting?

Louise No, she didn't; she missed it. She was incredibly disappointed about that, but apparently she jumped up and down in excitement when she heard that the painting had fetched nearly a million pounds.

Presenter Yes, that price is hardly surprising when you consider that the painting is one of the most popular prints ever made. Louise, thank you for joining us today.

Louise You're welcome.

8 A))

Presenter Hello and welcome to the programme. Today, we're looking at extraordinary medical conditions, and our first story concerns a young American girl called Ashlyn Blocker. Janice, tell us a bit about Ashlyn.

Janice Ashlyn Blocker has an extremely rare condition which means that she doesn't feel pain. Now, you might think that this would be a good thing, but in fact it can result in serious injury – or even death. To give you an example, Ashlyn can't feel extreme temperatures. So if she drops a spoon in boiling water while she's cooking, she simply puts her hand in the water to retrieve the spoon. She doesn't realize that she has burned herself until she sees that her fingers are red and swollen. This kind of thing happens to her almost daily.

Presenter I see the problem. So when did Ashlyn's parents notice that something wasn't quite right?

Janice Well, erm, as a baby, Ashlyn hardly ever cried, which is most unusual, and then when she was six months old, she didn't seem to notice when she had a serious cut on her eye. At first, the specialist thought that she had no feeling in the eye, and so he sent her to hospital for tests. Eighteen months later, the doctors gave Ashlyn's parents their diagnosis: she had 'congenital insensitivity to pain'.

Presenter Wow. What did her parents do then?

Janice Well, they didn't know what to do, so they just did their best to keep Ashlyn safe. They got rid of all of their furniture with sharp corners and lay down the softest carpet they could find. At school, teachers watched her all the time. One person was assigned to make sure that she was OK in the playground, and the nurse always checked her over before she went back to class. But even then, accidents happened, er, such as the time she broke her ankle and ran around on it for two days before her parents noticed.

Presenter Oh, how awful! Janice, how common is Ashlyn's condition?

Janice When it was first diagnosed, the doctors said that Ashlyn was the only person they had ever encountered who had it. Because the condition was so rare, there was very little on the internet. So Ashlyn's parents decided to go public to see if they could find anyone else like their daughter. First, they contacted their local newspaper, then the story was published nationally. Their story appeared in magazines, er on the, on the internet, and Ashlyn was interviewed on TV. All the media attention finally put the family in touch with scientists who could help them understand what was happening to Ashlyn.

Presenter What is it that causes the condition?

Janice It's a genetic disorder. Normally when we touch something hot or sharp, the nerves on the skin send electric signals to the brain, causing us to react. But in Ashlyn's case, there is a mutation in one of her genes. This alteration prevents communication between the nerves and the brain and so the electric signals are never produced.

Presenter Ashlyn sounds like a remarkable young woman, Janice; thank you for sharing her story with us. And now let's move on to someone else with an extraordinary medical condition…

8 B))

Normally when it snows in Atlanta, the temperature hovers around freezing, and nothing much ever happens 'cos the snow falls, but then the temperature goes up and everything melts and that's the end of it. But this time – oh my word! I mean it started snowing at about noon and immediately, really quickly the temperature dropped to -4, which is very unusual. I was in my office, which is up on the 51st floor, and I was getting kind of worried and I looked out on the streets and saw that nothing and no one was moving in any direction. And I live in a suburb, in Marietta, about 25 miles from the office in downtown Atlanta. So anyway at 5.30 two people, two of my co-workers who live near me, told me to hurry up and ride with them, so off we went.

Eight hours later, we had literally gone three miles, just three miles, and all along the side of the freeway people had parked because they were either too tired to go any further, or they had run out of gas. Several times we actually moved out of our lane, only to find that what had stopped the car in front of us from moving was that the driver had fallen asleep at the wheel!

I honestly didn't think we'd ever get home. I mean if we'd only gone three miles in eight hours, we might not be home for three days!

Anyway as the night wore on, I saw more and more people walking along the side of the freeway, and some of them were in high heels and thin jackets, and by this time it was, gosh, about -9. I have no idea where they were going because they were miles from anywhere.

Around 5.30 in the morning, like 12 hours after we'd left, we made it to the top of a hill, and all the way up the hill there were cars slipping and sliding, and huge trucks parked four or five parallel with the drivers sleeping, and people parked who were out of gas. It was just a thin stream of cars that was able to make it to the top of the hill, somehow sort of managing to get around all the cars that were slipping and sliding and crashing into each other. So fortunately we made it through, but we were going incredibly slowly.

And then, to our absolute amazement, the traffic thinned out and we were able to move a bit quicker. But we still had a problem. We were able to move, but we were on a thick sheet of ice, so every vehicle on the road was a potential weapon to all the others. We all had to keep our fingers crossed and drive slowly and hope no one would hit us. This continued for about 12 miles, at which point we had to go up a long hill at our exit. We had learned that hills were what did everybody in, what made them either crash or give up, and at our exit there were wrecks and empty cars and trucks everywhere, but we made it through and turned onto the road which leads to my house. It was just weird, really spooky, driving along that road for four miles at 6.45 in the morning without seeing a car or a person in any direction. I told the people I was with to drop me off on the main road because where I live is very hilly and I knew if they tried to get near the house, they'd never get away, so they let me out. But all I had on my feet was a pair of flat shoes, and I fell over seven times in quick succession until I realized that if I wanted to stop falling, I would have to walk the mile to my house in the deeper snow, on the side of the road. So up and down all those hills in my thin flat shoes I trudged through the snow and when I got near our house, I had to sit and slide down the hill! That was the only way I could get down there. I tell you I didn't know whether to laugh or cry. So, finally I stumbled in the door just as the sun was coming up at 7.30 in the morning, so it had taken me 14 hours! It really was something I'll never forget as long as I live.

9 A))

Speaker 1 Well, erm, we're both vegan, so I suppose that's a positive thing, cos we've got that in common. But I think Garfield definitely makes me less active than I used to be. He lives inside the house instead of outside in the garden, but, you know, I love having him around. Although he's quite big, he can still hop up onto the sofa, and aww, he likes to lie on my lap eating a carrot stick. Anyway, he usually ends up falling asleep, and he's so warm and soft, and aww, looking at him, I just don't want to disturb him, even when I've got things to do!

Speaker 2 I've had Philphil since she was a kitten, and I suppose we have one thing in common: we both enjoy harassing my husband. Philphil bites my husband's toes and attacks him on my behalf, constantly bothering him when he's trying to do something. Well in that sense, she's exactly like me! And, erm, well she shares my sense of humour. We both like to snuggle up at night as well. I can get very cold at night, and Philphil sleeps on the bed to keep me warm.

Speaker 3 People tell me that I'm eccentric, just like my pet, Molly. I suppose if enough people say it then it might be true. I'm sure I have picked up some of her traits, like the way I talk sometimes and bob my head, but erm I wouldn't say that I twittered. She does have several traits that I can see in myself, because Molly loves people, and at times she's a little bit of a show-off, just like me. And she's got a great sense of humour!

Speaker 4 I've had Crosby for what? Er, about eight years now – he's quite a rare breed, a Dandie Dinmont terrier. Oh, and yes, I think we look alike, yes. We've also developed the same personality over the years: I'm becoming a bit more bad-tempered, I think, and so is he, although he doesn't often bark. We both like our own space, and neither of us is as tolerant as we used to be. When it comes to food, I enjoy mine as much as he does, although, it has to be said, I'm a bit fussier.

Speaker 5 I keep reptiles, and I've noticed their personalities change to become more like mine. I've had bearded dragons calmly sitting and watching the telly when I do. If you've got lots of energy, they pick up on that, and if you're afraid, they are, too. They sort of tend to reflect whoever has brought them up. If they've had a stressed owner, for example, then they can be very stressed, they can behave like absolute lunatics, sometimes. But generally, because I'm calm, they tend to calm down themselves.

9 B)))

Speaker 1 Just after I left drama school, I was cooking supper for my boyfriend and another bloke who we were working with in the theatre, and I was going to do spaghetti bolognese and I wanted some green peppers. And I didn't realize then that there was a difference between green peppers and green chilli peppers, and so I cooked the spaghetti bolognese and I couldn't quite understand why my, underneath my nails was burning so terribly, but I just kept washing my hands and ignored it. And then we sat down to eat and Jeff, the friend who'd come, took one mouthful of the spaghetti bolognese before either of us did and fell off his chair onto the floor. And I'm afraid the whole lot had to go into the bin, it was the most horrendous experience.

Speaker 2 One particular one when I'd just bought a new oven, and I'd invited some friends round and I was going to cook a piece of roast meat, and I put it in my new oven, and turned it on and left it for an hour to cook. And when I opened the oven door, I realized that I'd put the grill on, not the oven, so that the top of the meat was completely charred, and underneath it was completely raw, so the meal was completely ruined. So I had to send out for a takeaway.

Speaker 3 Well, it didn't really involve cooking as such, but it was certainly a bad preparing food experience. My family, we went to Italy, and everybody in my family enjoyed the antipasti, the bruschetta, so I thought when I came home that I would re-invent this, you know it's very simple, basically it's little bits of bread with lovely tomato sauce on top and garlic. And I'd asked an Italian waiter and my Italian isn't very good, so I thought that I'd interpreted well what he'd said. However, you're supposed to rub the garlic on the bread, the sort of slightly toasted bread, just a little on one side. However, I went mad and was rubbing for a minute on both sides of the bread, and I put the tomato sauce on and handed it to my family, and they all spat it out, it was inedible. I think we threw it away.

10 A)))

Presenter Hello and welcome to the show. There are many stories about immigrants coming to the UK and today we're going to look at some of the best. Our starting point is a novel by the Bangladeshi-born British writer Monica Ali. It's called *Brick Lane*, and here's Jenny Trench to tell us about it.

Jenny Hello there. *Brick Lane* tells the story of Nazneen, a Bangladeshi woman, who is sent to England at the age of 18 to enter into an arranged marriage. Her husband is Chanu, a middle-aged civil servant, who is also a Bangladeshi immigrant. Nazneen has been told that Chanu is a successful man, because this is how her father and his peers regard Bangladeshis who have left the country to make a new life for themselves abroad. But Chanu is not a success. He lives on a relatively poor housing estate in an area of London called Tower Hamlets and his apartment is not only full of ugly furniture, but is also in need of repair. Nazneen is confused by her new husband and her new surroundings, and to make things worse, she's forbidden from leaving the house. At first she accepts her fate and settles into the traditional role of wife and mother, while still an outsider in London.

Presenter Jenny, apart from Nazneen, tell us about the other characters in the story.

Jenny Well, I've already mentioned Chanu, Nazneen's husband. He is full of endless plans to become successful, but he's incapable of realizing any of them. At first, Nazneen has a positive aversion to him, but as time goes by, they gradually begin to accept one another. Then, there are the two daughters, Shanana and Bibi. Shanana battles constantly with her father, mainly because she prefers British culture, while Bibi longs for stability. Nazneen's sister Hasina appears often in the story in the many letters she sends, describing her troubled life back in Bangladesh. Hasina's fate is quite the opposite to Nazneen's as she eloped to make a love marriage and then ran away when her husband began beating her. Razia, Nazneen's unconventional friend, who shaves her head and wears European clothes, often visits Nazneen for a chat. And of course there is Karim, the good-looking young man who is Nazneen's lover for a time.

Presenter Of course. What did you like most about the story, Jenny?

Jenny The thing I liked most was the way we see Nazneen begin to take control of her life. Nazneen was taught from birth to accept her fate, and this is what she does on her arrival in England. As time passes, however, she begins to question the role of fate. One day, she leaves the house to explore the neighbourhood and comes across Brick Lane itself, a street which is the very heart of London's Bangladeshi community. As her daughters grow, she learns English from them, which allows her to function in the world outside her home. Her life opens up more when she starts taking in sewing to earn some extra money and she meets Karim. But *Brick Lane* is not a love story. It's about Nazneen's development as a person. In the closing pages, we find a much more confident Nazneen. We are aware that her troubles are not over, but we know that she's much better-equipped to cope with them than she was when she first arrived in London.

Presenter Thank you, Jenny Trench. So that was Monica Ali's novel, *Brick Lane*. And now on to our next book…

10 B)))

Presenter A question that many parents ask themselves is when they should introduce their children to a sport. If rugby coach Joseph Ting is to be believed, the answer is: as soon as possible. Two years ago, Ting and his colleague Luke Walden founded Rugby Munchkins, a rugby club for toddlers. Players can join from the tender age of two. This is what rugby dad Ollie Sampson has to say about his daughter's experience of the club.

Dad Chloë is three and nearing the end of her first season as a rugby player. She's always been quite a physical, outgoing kind of girl, and she loves her Sunday morning classes, charging around with a ball in her hands, though usually not in the direction the coaches want her to go. Tackling is what she likes best, and if you stand a large, stuffed, orange tackle bag in front of her, she'll bring it crashing to the ground. I think she could be a pretty good player if she sticks at it.

Presenter Believe it or not, the motto of the programme is 'gently introducing children to rugby'. We asked one of the coaches to tell us how this theory works in practice.

Coach With the youngest ones, we get them to run across the field with a ball. When they put the ball down everyone shouts 'try' and claps. As they get older, we introduce them to new games, like Hungry Munchkins. This is a game which teaches them speed, ball-handling, colour identification, and, perhaps the hardest lesson of all, to stand in line and wait for their turn. The children are in four teams: red, blue, green, and yellow. In the middle of the pitch, there is a pile of coloured balls. Players take it in turns to collect their team's coloured balls from the pile and bring them back to a basket. We play lots of games like this, and all of our games are educational as well as physical.

Presenter It has recently been reported that two-thirds of children would rather that sports were not competitive. So we asked how much emphasis Rugby Munchkins puts on success and failure.

Coach We aim to teach the children that you can keep score without it being everything. They all understand that the process of scoring a try gives their team points but we don't make a thing about winning. After a match, everyone gets a sticker, not just the winning team.

Presenter It'll be interesting to see how many of the current Munchkins are still playing in the future. You never know, one of them might make the national team, which will show that Ting and Walden's efforts have been worthwhile.

Answer key

1A

1 GRAMMAR

a 2 doesn't have / hasn't got
3 Did you have
4 Do you have / Have you got
5 had
6 had had
7 didn't have to
8 won't have

b 2 doesn't have to
3 have, had
4 haven't got / don't have / haven't
5 'm having
6 hasn't been
7 Did, have
8 do, have / have, got

2 VOCABULARY

a 2 sarcastic
3 conscientious
4 resourceful
5 thorough
6 sympathetic
7 gentle
8 straightforward

b 2 seems
3 taken
4 tends / tries
5 refused
6 take

c 2 a pain in the neck
3 has a (very) quick temper
4 a cold fish
5 down to earth
6 a soft touch

3 PRONUNCIATION

a 2 consci<u>e</u>ntious
3 <u>cu</u>rious
4 de<u>te</u>rmined
5 <u>ge</u>ntle
6 self-suffi<u>c</u>ient
7 <u>stea</u>dy
8 re<u>sour</u>ceful
9 sar<u>ca</u>stic
10 spont<u>a</u>neous
11 sympa<u>the</u>tic
12 <u>tho</u>rough

4 LEXIS IN CONTEXT

2 stuck
3 together
4 eye
5 round
6 gut
7 head
8 off
9 white

5 LISTENING

a They mention more advantages.

b A 3 B 2 C 4 D 1

6 READING

a Sentence 1 is the best.

b 1 c 2 b 3 d 4 a 5 c 6 b

1B

1 LEXIS IN CONTEXT

2 head
3 keep
4 looks
5 blank
6 build
7 heart
8 wearing

2 VOCABULARY

a 2 rewarding
3 demanding
4 promoted
5 employ
6 made redundant
7 monotonous
8 off work
9 perks
10 hire

b 2 full-time
3 job-hunting
4 academic qualifications
5 career ladder
6 events management
7 permanent contract
8 clocking off
9 apply for a position

3 GRAMMAR

a 2 Consequently
3 Even though
4 because
5 not to
6 due to
7 nevertheless
8 in case

b 2 so as not to forget the time
3 as a result, it will be closed until further notice
4 due to the late arrival of the incoming plane
5 despite not meeting all the requirements
6 so that they would be ready for the exam the next day
7 in spite of not being able to go to the interview / in spite of the fact that she wasn't able to go to the interview
8 owing to his illness / owing to the fact that he was ill

4 LEXIS IN CONTEXT

2 ploy
3 issue
4 travel-focused
5 workload
6 tackle

5 PRONUNCIATION

a 2 <u>free</u>lance
3 <u>tem</u>porary
4 <u>vo</u>luntary
5 com<u>pa</u>ssionate
6 ma<u>ter</u>nity
7 <u>per</u>manent
8 <u>mo</u>tivating
9 mo<u>no</u>tonous
10 aca<u>de</u>mic
11 <u>ma</u>nagement
12 qualifi<u>ca</u>tions

c 1 event
2 quit
3 perks
4 benefits

6 READING

a He would say it was fiction.

b 1 E 2 B 3 F 4 A 5 D

c 1 jam-packed
2 somewhere along the line
3 plain sailing
4 was up to
5 is another matter
6 jump at the chance

7 LISTENING

a The man would love to be a travel writer and would hate a job on a production line.

b 1 The man thinks he would be good at the first job because he thinks he is quite sociable, is a good writer, he doesn't mind living out of a suitcase, he can live cheap, and it would be a wonderful way to see the world.
2 A downside might be that you would have to write a book, even if you had nothing to say.
3 He thinks he would hate the second job because he wouldn't have to think and it would be very repetitive.
4 He did a job of this kind when he was 18, but he didn't like it.

Talking about...work and family

1 LOOKING AT LANGUAGE

2 Apparently
3 as to
4 in a way
5 basically
6 really
7 I mean
8 anyway

2 READING

a 1 D 2 F 3 A 4 E 5 B

2A

1 LEXIS IN CONTEXT

2 fluid
3 part
4 random
5 guidance

2 PRONUNCIATION

a 3 S
4 S
5 D
6 S
7 D
8 D
9 S
10 D

3 GRAMMAR

a 2 ✗ talking to each other / one another
3 ✓
4 ✗ we should help ourselves
5 ✗ When a guest leaves their room
6 ✗ by myself / on my own
7 ✗ so far below her
8 ✓

b 2 myself
3 each other / one another
4 One
5 yourself
6 They
7 herself
8 you / one

c 2 it
3 There
4 it
5 There
6 there
7 There
8 there
9 It
10 it

4 VOCABULARY

a 2 take in
3 tell
4 pick up
5 say
6 get by
7 talk
8 brush up

b 2 requested
3 error
4 respond to
5 tongue

c 2 the wrong end of the stick
3 on the tip of my tongue
4 at cross purposes
5 get my head round

5 READING

a How the language is constructed, culture, and the way objects are classified

b 1 D 2 G 3 A 4 E 5 B 6 H

c 1 derogatory
2 formulate
3 concur
4 versus
5 determine
6 addressed
7 revealing

6 LISTENING

b 1 Do you find it easier to understand native or non-native speakers of English?
2 How do you feel about having your English corrected?
3 Do you have any funny or embarrassing stories related to misunderstanding someone?
4 Is there anything you still find difficult about English?

c 1 M 2 B 3 M 4 W 5 W 6 B

2B

1 LEXIS IN CONTEXT

2 rushing
3 bubbling away
4 slapped
5 concocting
6 picture
7 leap

2 GRAMMAR

a 3 ✗ had forgotten to
4 ✗ would catch / used to catch / caught
5 ✗ broke down
6 ✓
7 ✗ lived / used to live
8 ✗ I'd been hiding
9 ✗ were still working
10 ✓

b 2 shared / used to share
3 went / used to go
4 had cleaned
5 would lie / used to lie
6 fell
7 had been singing
8 stopped
9 stood
10 looked
11 was staring
12 told
13 was watching
14 had seen
15 didn't sleep

3 VOCABULARY

a 2 fear
3 improvement
4 hatred
5 death
6 belief
7 shame

b 2 wisdom
3 childhood
4 sadness
5 celebration
6 membership
7 illness
8 boredom

4 PRONUNCIATION

a Circle *celebration*, *imagination*, and *curiosity*

5 LISTENING

a Speaker 4

b A 3 B 1 C 4 D 2 E 5
F 1 G 5 H 4 I 2 J 3

6 READING

a 9/10

b 1 T 2 F 3 F 4 F 5 T 6 F

3A

1 PRONUNCIATION

a 2 rendezvous
3 faux pas
4 déjà vu
5 entrepreneur
6 ballet
7 bouquet
8 fiancé(e)
9 coup
10 fait accompli

2 VOCABULARY

a 2 f
3 e
4 d
5 g
6 b
7 a
8 c
9 h

b 2 message
  3 way
  4 anywhere
  5 life
  6 on
  7 house
  8 act
c 2 around / round
  3 away
  4 behind
  5 out
  6 down
  7 on
  8 through
  9 by
  10 back

3 LEXIS IN CONTEXT
  2 rule out
  3 win, over
  4 foot, bill
  5 short, sweet
  6 miss out
  7 follow, through
  8 make up, mind

4 GRAMMAR
  2 Can you get Paul to look at my computer?
  3 I'll never get used to getting up at 5.30 in the morning.
  4 The afternoon shadows got longer as the sun went down.
  5 We're getting our kitchen repainted next month.
  6 I can't get the kids to eat their dinner.
  7 I hope I don't get sent to Manchester – I want to stay in London.
  8 Public transport in my town is getting better.
  9 My boss got fired for stealing money.
  10 Could you possibly get Mike to pick me up?

5 LISTENING
a Speakers 2, 4 and 5 had successful dates. Speakers 1 and 3 had unsuccessful dates.
b 1 F 2 F 3 T 4 F 5 F 6 T
  7 T 8 T 9 F 10 F

6 READING
a Number 5 caused the most damage.
b 1 H 2 C 3 D 4 E 5 F 6 B

1 VOCABULARY
a Across: 3 spear
    5 cannon
    6 bow
    8 shield
    9 bullet
  Down: 2 machine gun
    3 sword
    4 arrow

---

    7 missile
b 2 casualties
  3 declared
  4 shelled
  5 ceasefire
  6 surrender
  7 defeated
  8 snipers
  9 looted
  10 commander

2 PRONUNCIATION
a 2 civil
  3 refugee
  4 survivor
  5 commander
  6 ceasefire
  7 victory
  8 release
  9 capture
  10 retreat
  11 execute
  12 surrender
c 1 shield
  2 bullet
  3 weapon
  4 declare

3 GRAMMAR
a 2 words
  3 concerned
  4 matter
  5 whole
  6 way
  7 say
  8 case
  9 hand
  10 least
b 2 Basically
  3 I mean
  4 Besides
  5 Obviously
  6 all in all
  7 After all
  8 As I was saying
  9 To sum up
  10 otherwise

4 LISTENING
a 1 b 2 d 3 a 4 e 5 c
b 1 E 2 C 3 G 4 A 5 D

5 READING
a 1 b 2 d 3 a 4 e 5 c
b 2 D
  3 A
  4 E
  5 C
  6 A
  7 D
  8 C
  9 B
  10 E

---

c 1 ill fate
  2 charged
  3 moulding
  4 slaughtered
  5 mercilessly
  6 morale
  7 pass
  8 pivotal

Colloquial English
Talking about...history

1 LOOKING AT LANGUAGE
  2 awful
  3 deadly
  4 rights
  5 picture
  6 classic
  7 civil
  8 ordinary

2 READING
a 1 T
  2 F
  3 F
  4 T
  5 F
  6 T
  7 T
  8 F

4A

1 VOCABULARY
a 2 tapping
  3 bang
  4 slurp
  5 rattling
  6 hissed
  7 roared
  8 sniffing
  9 crunched
  10 ticking
  11 screeching
  12 slammed
b 2 sighed
  3 sobbed
  4 groaned
  5 screamed
  6 stammered
  7 whispered
  8 giggled
  9 mumbled

2 PRONUNCIATION
a 2 stretch
  3 exclaimed
  4 sixth
  5 shelves
  6 bridegroom
  7 spread
  8 punched

3 LEXIS IN CONTEXT

2 continually
3 with ease
4 Strangely
5 in, proximity
6 seemingly
7 incessantly

4 GRAMMAR

a 2 could / might / may be waiting
  3 should have been
  4 might / may not like
  5 can't be studying
  6 might / may not have taken
  7 can't have
  8 must / might have forgotten

b 2 're bound to win the match
  3 'll definitely enjoy the film
  4 's not likely to rain tonight
  5 're unlikely to agree to our proposal
  6 will probably take early retirement
  7 are sure to complain about it
  8 definitely won't give us a pay rise

5 LISTENING

a She is deaf.

b 1 20
  2 60
  3 soundtracks
  4 hearing / deafness
  5 feeling
  6 shoes

6 READING

a In a hospital.

b 1 T
  2 T
  3 F
  4 F
  5 F
  6 T
  7 T

c 1 background, ambient
  2 jingle
  3 din

1 VOCABULARY

2 thought-provoking
3 entertaining
4 implausible
5 intriguing
6 depressing
7 gripping
8 heavy-going
9 moving
10 fast-moving

2 PRONUNCIATION

a 2 walk
  3 implausible
  4 resourceful
  5 rewarding
  6 daughter
  7 thought-provoking
  8 workforce

c 1 I bought his autobiography from the store.
  2 The crowd roared when the captain scored.
  3 Your lawyer talks more when he's in court.
  4 He was caught by enemy forces in the war.
  5 That story is awfully boring.

3 GRAMMAR

a 2 Not until
  3 Rarely
  4 No sooner
  5 Only
  6 Scarcely / Hardly
  7 Not only
  8 Never

b 2 did he betray my trust, but he also wrecked my car.
  3 had the sun gone down when / before the temperature fell dramatically.
  4 have I seen such a wonderful sight.
  5 had the teacher turned her back than the children started whispering.
  6 had the woman sat down when / before her baby started crying.
  7 do you find two people so alike.
  8 a replacement teacher has been found will classes recommence.

4 LEXIS IN CONTEXT

2 identical
3 implored
4 mute
5 immobile
6 done with
7 merely
8 accurate
9 backpacks
10 conceivable

5 LISTENING

a 1 successful
  2 not successful

b 1 F 2 T 3 T 4 F 5 T 6 F

6 READING

a The author advises not to try to finish a book if you're really not enjoying it.

b 1 c 2 b 3 a 4 c 5 c

c 1 grab you
  2 take a shine to
  3 put you off
  4 for pity's sake
  5 to its bitter end
  6 out of hand

1 LEXIS IN CONTEXT

2 with
3 of
4 of
5 with
6 on

2 GRAMMAR

a 2 appears
  3 expected
  4 According
  5 may
  6 seem
  7 agreed
  8 Apparently

b 2 It appears / It would appear that
  3 It has been announced
    It was announced that
  4 is thought to have
  5 may have been
  6 It seems / It would seem that
  7 might have entered
  8 It is hoped that

3 VOCABULARY

a 2 saved
  3 takes
  4 spare
  5 make
  6 gave
  7 having
  8 ran

b 2 From, to
  3 at
  4 on
  5 In
  6 by
  7 before
  8 at

c 2 short
  3 spare
  4 hands
  5 being
  6 matter
  7 up
  8 whole

4 PRONUNCIATION

a 2 My cousin‿Nick‿is never‿on time.
  3 I find‿doing housework takes‿up‿a lot‿of time.
  4 We walked‿to town‿as we had plenty‿of time.
  5 We seem to have run‿out‿of time.
  6 It's‿a question‿of time before the sports‿centre opens.

c 1 I always freak out if the bus arrives late.
  2 He's a bit impatient at times.
  3 We stood in the queue for over an hour.
  4 You'll have to wait a moment until I'm ready.
  5 The performance starts at 8 o'clock.
  6 She's awfully insecure about their relationship.

5 LISTENING

a The good news is that it's possible to slow time down.

b 1 senses
   2 longer
   3 new
   4 slowly
   5 familiar
   6 quickly
   7 learning
   8 new places
   9 new people
   10 spontaneous

6 READING

a The writer thinks that being late is rude.

b 1 c 2 b 3 c 4 d 5 a

c 1 a 2 c 3 b 4 b

d 1 superiority
   2 behaviour
   3 lateness
   4 belief
   5 absence

5B

1 LEXIS IN CONTEXT

   2 collide
   3 shoulders
   4 littered with
   5 juggle
   6 high-flying

2 GRAMMAR

a 2 I'd rather you came round
   3 I wish we hadn't bought
   4 If only we lived
   5 I'd rather she didn't know.
   6 If only I'd worked
   7 It's time you had
   8 I wish we were

b 2 If only we didn't owe
   3 It's time Sally made up
   4 Would you rather we took
   5 If only we hadn't spent
   6 it time you apologized
   7 I wish I were able to see
   8 We'd rather you didn't

3 VOCABULARY

a 2 stock market
   3 exchange rate
   4 in debt
   5 standard, living
   6 inflation
   7 consumer society
   8 Interest rates
   9 grant
   10 donation

b 2 penniless, P
   3 loaded, R
   4 hard up, P
   5 wealthy, R
   6 well-off, R
   7 broke, P

c 2 in the red
   3 doesn't grow on trees
   4 cost an arm and a leg
   5 we tighten our belts
   6 daylight robbery
   7 tight-fisted
   8 make ends meet

4 PRONUNCIATION

a 2 US
   3 UK
   4 US
   5 UK
   6 UK
   7 US
   8 UK
   9 UK
   10 US

5 LISTENING

a 1 Philip
   2 Wendy
   3 Emily
   4 Mary
   5 Jonathan

b 1 18°C
   2 a packed lunch
   3 in a jar
   4 in cash
   5 when you're hungry / on an empty stomach

6 READING

a C

b 1 C 2 A 3 F 4 B 5 E

Colloquial English

Talking about...stress and relaxation

1 LOOKING AT LANGUAGE

   2 age group
   3 blood pressure
   4 support network
   5 text messages
   6 breathing exercises
   7 life saver
   8 college students

2 READING

a 1 b 2 b 3 a 4 c 5 b

6A

1 LEXIS IN CONTEXT

   2 belief
   3 cool
   4 hand
   5 stressing
   6 squirrel
   7 stomach
   8 mode

2 GRAMMAR

a 2 c
   3 a
   4 c
   5 b
   6 a
   7 a
   8 b

b 2 her not to tell
   3 you to come / that you come
   4 them to get
   5 you working
   6 him (to) overcome
   7 me not paying
   8 them to arrive

3 VOCABULARY

a 2 conscious
   3 hand
   4 minute
   5 minded

b 2 dead-end
   3 high-pitched
   4 feel-good
   5 life-changing
   6 low-cost
   7 ground-breaking
   8 labour-saving
   9 eco-friendly
   10 hands-free

4 PRONUNCIATION

a 2 high-<u>risk</u>
   3 home-<u>made</u>
   4 last-<u>minute</u>
   5 long-<u>distance</u>
   6 narrow-<u>minded</u>
   7 second-<u>hand</u>
   8 self-<u>conscious</u>
   9 well-be<u>haved</u>
   10 worn-<u>out</u>

5 LISTENING

a 1 S 2 W 3 S 4 S 5 W 6 W

b 1 F 2 T 3 T 4 F 5 T 6 F 7 F

6 READING

a 2

b 1 D 2 G 3 A 4 E 5 C

c 1 plausibly
   2 gloomily
   3 widely
   4 presumably
   5 demonstrably
   6 indisputably

6B

1 VOCABULARY

a 2 charge
3 landline
4 signal
5 give
6 engaged
7 tone
8 reception
9 missed

b 2 c
3 b
4 c
5 a
6 b
7 c
8 a
9 b
10 c

c 2 Wi-fi
3 keypad
4 Streaming
5 passcode
6 An update
7 contacts
8 touch screen

2 LEXIS IN CONTEXT

2 albeit
3 wolf
4 justification
5 plausibility
6 decent
7 negotiation
8 donned

3 PRONUNCIATION

a 2 b
3 a
4 b
5 a
6 a
7 a
8 b
9 a
10 b

4 GRAMMAR

a 2 won't be able
3 hadn't been snoring
4 didn't come
5 Would, change
6 hadn't eaten
7 would have called
8 wouldn't owe

b 2 Had we known you were at home
3 Supposing you missed your flight, what would you do
4 whether they like it or not
5 Provided you look after my bike
6 even if we can't afford it
7 on condition (that) she finishes the report by the weekend
8 as long as they didn't make too much noise

5 VOCABULARY

2 g *of / with*
3 d *to*
4 f *on*
5 b *with*
6 a *to*
7 c *on*

6 LISTENING

a 1 organizing things alphabetically
2 the internet / chatting online
3 cleaning
4 shopping
5 counting things

b A 3 B 1 C 4 D 5 E 2

7 READING

a 1 c 2 e 3 b 4 a 5 f 6 d

b 1 D
2 E
3 B
4 C
5 A
6 F
7 F
8 D
9 C
10 A
11 E
12 B

c 1 trawl
2 track
3 divert
4 synch
5 split
6 swipe
7 post
8 withdraw

7A

1 PRONUNCIATION

a ✓ 3, 4, 6, 8

c 2 What‿a tragic‿end!
3 What‿a nice‿surprise!
4 What‿a sad‿ending!
5 What‿an‿awful thing to happen!
6 What‿a horrible story!
7 What‿a lovely day!

2 VOCABULARY

a 2 inhospitable
3 illiterate
4 irrational
5 incompetent
6 discontinued
7 impersonal
8 unofficial

b 2 anti-smoking
3 overcharge
4 updated
5 rescheduled
6 demotivating
7 outplayed
8 prematurely
9 ill-advised
10 underestimated

3 LEXIS IN CONTEXT

2 limped
3 imposed
4 confiscated
5 cited
6 reinforced
7 interfered
8 grimaced
9 calmed
10 beeped

4 GRAMMAR

a 2 shouldn't
3 must have
4 don't have to
5 needn't
6 mustn't
7 We're allowed to
8 couldn't
9 can

b 2 shouldn't have bought
3 wasn't allowed to / wasn't able to wear
4 are supposed to speak English
5 had/'d better not be
6 won't be able to come
7 ought to apply
8 needn't have taken
9 It is not permitted to use

5 LISTENING

a Both positive and negative.

b 1 T 2 F 3 T 4 F 5 T 6 T

6 READING

a 1 D 2 A 3 B 4 F

b 1 b
2 c
3 a
4 c
5 a
6 a
7 b
8 a

c 1 cautious
2 to the contrary
3 legislation
4 in effect
5 in authority

1 GRAMMAR

a 2 saw
3 've / have, heard
4 smells
5 doesn't feel
6 looked
7 don't sound
8 seems

b 2 see that waiter drop
3 seems to have lost
4 doesn't sound like
5 looks exactly like
6 heard the baby crying
7 seems / looks as if we are
8 sounds like
9 can smell (something)

2 PRONUNCIATION

a 2 endure
3 allure
4 nature
5 sure
6 immature

3 VOCABULARY

Across: 5 self-portrait
6 landscape
Down: 2 sculpture
3 portrait
4 still-life

4 LEXIS IN CONTEXT

2 couple
3 later
4 within
5 until
6 few

5 VOCABULARY

2 red herring
3 out of the blue
4 in black and white
5 grey area
6 red tape
7 black market
8 white lie

6 LISTENING

a The artist.

b 1 She was 17.
2 She was working in her uncle's laundry.
3 Yes, she had read about him in the newspaper.
4 The real gown was blue, but the one in the painting is yellow.
5 She thought about the traumas he had experienced in his life.
6 He paid her just over six South African pounds.
7 She didn't like her green face or the title.
8 She got married, moved to Johannesburg, and had five children.
9 She was very excited.

7 READING

a 2

b 1 C 2 A 3 F 4 D 5 B

Talking about…illustration

1 LOOKING AT LANGUAGE

2 way
3 work
4 kind
5 number
6 age
7 mood

2 READING

a 1 They work together to produce a single work of art.
2 While they were at university.
3 The editors got confused because they were identical twins.
4 They are special editions illustrated by professional artists.
5 To bear children for other couples.
6 They could see their own story in it.
7 The accentuated perspectives, strong light and the use of few colours.
8 It won a gold medal for being the best illustration of 2012.

1 VOCABULARY

a 2 faint
3 X-ray
4 surgeon
5 scan
6 cold
7 plaster
8 bruise
9 asthma
Hidden word: diagnosis

b 2 electric shock
3 blister
4 allergic reaction
5 flu
6 antibiotics
7 stitches
8 heart attack
9 rash
10 food poisoning

2 LEXIS IN CONTEXT

2 nothing
3 risk(s)
4 heart
5 word

3 GRAMMAR

a 2 to programme
3 to be sniffing
4 being photographed
5 complaining
6 to become
7 have worn
8 taking
9 to set up
10 Having learnt

b 2 to have paid
3 to have met
4 enough to swim
5 to have lost
6 to be made
7 to be chosen
8 being taken to
9 Having read the
10 nowhere to go
11 no point inviting

4 LEXIS IN CONTEXT

2 makes
3 do
4 make
5 does
6 did
7 Making

5 VOCABULARY

2 stubborn
3 white
4 good
5 drinks
6 quick
7 sleep
8 thin
9 deaf
10 blind

6 PRONUNCIATION

a Circled words in **bold**:
2 **The** surgeon arrived **as** soon **as the** patient **was** ready.
3 It **was** too late **for a** doctor, so we went straight **to** hospital.
4 **The** specialist suggested I went on **a** diet **for a** while.
5 I'm allergic **to** plasters, so I never use **them**.

b 2 The sur<u>geo</u>n arrived as soon as the pati<u>e</u>nt was ready.
3 It was too late for a doc<u>to</u>r, so we went straight to hosp<u>i</u>tal.
4 The spec<u>ia</u>list s<u>ugg</u>ested I went on a di<u>e</u>t for a while.
5 I'm <u>a</u>llergic to pla<u>ste</u>rs, so I ne<u>ve</u>r use <u>them</u>.

7 READING

a 3

b 1 a 2 c 3 b 4 a

8 LISTENING

a Ashlyn doesn't feel pain. Her condition is a genetic disorder.

b 1 F
  2 T
  3 T
  4 T
  5 F
  6 F
  7 T
  8 F

8B

1 VOCABULARY

a 2 cancel
  3 get
  4 postpone
  5 wander / walk
  6 extend
  7 set
  8 go
  9 hit
  10 recharge
  11 sample
  12 chill
  13 soak

b 2 spoilt
  3 remote
  4 tacky
  5 unspoilt
  6 dull
  7 lively
  8 overrated
  9 picturesque
  10 overcrowded
  11 breathtaking
  12 off the beaten track

2 LEXIS IN CONTEXT

2 a
3 a
4 c
5 b
6 c
7 c
8 b

3 GRAMMAR

a 2 ✓
  3 on the point of leaving
  4 Will you be eating
  5 ✓
  6 I won't be driving
  7 ✓
  8 ✓
  9 I'm about to go

b 2 is due to land
  3 will be picking me up
  4 on the point of
  5 leaves at
  6 is about to start
  7 am / 'm taking part
  8 is to be held

4 LEXIS IN CONTEXT

2 height
3 bumpy
4 relieved
5 approaching
6 circled
7 off
8 turbulence
9 dilemma
10 winds

5 PRONUNCIATION

2 a
3 b
4 b
5 a
6 a
7 b
8 a
9 b
10 a

6 READING

a Summary 3 is correct.

b 1 D 2 A 3 F 4 H 5 C 6 B

7 LISTENING

a 14 hours

b 1 It was incredibly cold / -4°degrees.
  2 It's 25 miles away.
  3 Two of her co-workers / colleagues.
  4 Because they were tired or they had run out of gas / petrol.
  5 They were wearing high heels and thin jackets.
  6 There were a lot of cars slipping and sliding, and trucks parked by the road. They had to go incredibly slowly. They were on a thick sheet of ice. They had to go up a long hill.
  7 On the main road.
  8 In the deep snow at the side of the road.
  9 She sat and slid down the hill.
  10 It was 7.30 in the morning.

9A

1 LEXIS IN CONTEXT

2 adores
3 content
4 care
5 sceptical
6 live

2 VOCABULARY

a 2 squeak
  3 neigh
  4 shell
  5 chick
  6 calves
  7 cage
  8 claws
Hidden word: beehives

b 2 horns, dog
  3 fur, bird
  4 beak, cat
  5 grunt, fish
  6 twitter, pig

c 2 bred, captivity
  3 rights activists
  4 hunted, sport
  5 endangered species
  6 charity, protect, environment
  7 live, wild
  8 treated cruelly

3 GRAMMAR

a 2 d
  3 e
  4 a
  5 g ✓
  6 i
  7 c ✓
  8 b
  9 h ✓

b 2 might
  3 do
  4 should
  5 wouldn't
  6 couldn't
  7 isn't
  8 was
  9 won't

c 2 so
  3 to
  4 not
  5 so
  6 to
  7 not
  8 to

4 PRONUNCIATION

a A Do you know where you're going on holiday yet?
  B No, I don't. I'd love to go on a safari, but my girlfriend doesn't want to.
  A She doesn't like animals, does she?
  B She does like animals – she's got three cats. But she doesn't want to go on a safari.
  A Where does she want to go then? Doesn't she want to see lions in the wild? I'd love to.
  B So would I. And so would my girlfriend. But she really doesn't like camping. Neither do I if I'm honest.

5 LISTENING

a 1 rabbit
  2 cat
  3 parrot
  4 dog
  5 lizard

b A 4 B 2 C 1 D 5 E 3

6 READING

a Numbers 2 and 4 are not mentioned.

b 1 E 2 C 3 D 4 A 5 F

1 VOCABULARY

a 2 sliced
3 toasted
4 chopped
5 whipped
6 scrambled
7 minced
8 deep-fried
9 steamed
10 grilled

b 2 food processor
3 colander
4 baking tray
5 whisk
6 mixing bowl
7 sieve
8 chopping board
9 frying pan
10 saucepan

2 PRONUNCIATION

a 2 comfortable
3 medicine
4 different
5 temperature
6 chocolate
7 dictionary
8 vegetables

3 LEXIS IN CONTEXT

2 fiddly
3 stuff
4 gobble
5 chew

4 GRAMMAR

a 3 ✓
4 ✓
5 ✓
6 ✗ cereal bowl
7 ✓
8 ✗ the end of the story
9 ✗ plastic bags
10 ✓

b 2 women's magazines
3 vegetable drawer
4 Fiona and Charles' / Charles's car
5 trainee manager
6 husband's clothes
7 bread knife
8 animals' cages
9 alarm clock

5 LEXIS IN CONTEXT

2 Chillies
3 Ginger
4 Monkfish
5 Oysters

6 LISTENING

a No.

b Speaker 1:
1 She was cooking for her boyfriend and a friend.
2 She was making spaghetti bolognese.
3 She used chilli peppers instead of green peppers.
4 She threw the dish in the bin.

Speaker 2:
1 He was cooking for friends.
2 He was cooking a piece of roast meat.
3 He put the grill on instead of the oven.
4 He ordered a takeaway.

Speaker 3:
1 She was cooking for her family.
2 She was preparing antipasti (bruschetta).
3 She used too much garlic.
4 She threw the food away.

7 READING

a Heading 3 is the best alternative.

b 1 c 2 b 3 a 4 c 5 d 6 b

Colloquial English

Talking about...insects and animals

1 LOOKING AT LANGUAGE

2 bit
3 whole
4 like
5 pretty
6 so
7 went
8 there
9 going
10 something

2 READING

a 1 F 2 T 3 T 4 F 5 T 6 T

10A

1 LEXIS IN CONTEXT

2 ruled
3 back
4 hurdle
5 nothing
6 detox
7 stumbled
8 ball

2 GRAMMAR

a 2 d
3 g
4 f
5 a
6 b
7 c
8 e

b 2 The person I spoke to was the assistant manager, not the manager.
3 The reason (why) I didn't buy the bag was because / that it was too expensive.
4 It was her grandmother who taught her how to bake bread.
5 What happened was (that) Jane shut the door with her keys still inside.
6 What I need is a good, long rest.
7 The thing that impressed me was / I was impressed by was how quickly she learnt Italian.
8 The village where my parents live / my parents live in is very picturesque.

3 PRONUNCIATION

a 1 The thing I like most about my husband is his sense of humour.
2 What I don't understand is why you didn't tell me before.
3 The reason why I don't like cheese is because of the texture.
4 It was the lorry that caused the accident.
5 The person I'd most like to go on holiday with is my sister.
6 It's your health that I'm worried about.

4 LEXIS IN CONTEXT

2 On
3 acquiring
4 proceedings
5 dispiriting
6 gravely
7 entered
8 reflecting
9 seek
10 melancholy

5 VOCABULARY

a 2 refuse
3 lie
4 commitment
5 economical
6 suite
7 besides
8 currently
9 embarrassed
10 affects

b 2 beside
3 economic
4 lay
5 ashamed
6 effects
7 actually
8 suit
9 compromise
10 deny

6 LISTENING

a In general, the book has a happy ending.

b 1 T
   2 T
   3 F
   4 F
   5 T
   6 F
   7 T
   8 F

7 READING

a Sentence 2 is the best.

b 1 b   2 d   3 a   4 c   5 b

10B

1 LEXIS IN CONTEXT

2 sit-ups
3 thighs
4 vigorous
5 spine
6 training
7 flexibility
8 press-ups
9 stretch
10 trunk

2 VOCABULARY

2 height
3 flatten
4 shorten
5 strength
6 depth
7 weakened
8 lengthen
9 width

3 GRAMMAR

a 2 where
   3 of which
   4 whose
   5 which, –
   6 which
   7 that, which, –
   8 what
   9 who
   10 to whom

b 2 My cousin, who is a cross-country runner, has been given a scholarship by an American University.
   3 There's been a frost, which means that the match will probably be cancelled.
   4 Our team has two goalkeepers, neither of whom can play next weekend.
   5 These trainers, which I've only had for a week, have broken already.
   6 We spoke to a steward, who directed us to our seats.
   7 The racket (which / that) I bought for my son wasn't very expensive.
   8 The showers, many of which do not work properly, are very rarely cleaned.

4 PRONUNCIATION

a 2 a, b
   3 a, b
   4 b, a
   5 a, b
   6 a, b
   7 b, a

5 LISTENING

a The children are learning how to play rugby, and the classes aren't very competitive.

b 1 founders
   2 two
   3 boys and girls
   4 Sunday
   5 physical
   6 games
   7 four
   8 sticker

6 READING

a 2 Short periods of exercise.

b 1 E   2 C   3 A   4 G   5 B   6 F

UNIVERSITY PRESS

Great Clarendon Street, Oxford, OX2 6DP, United Kingdom

Oxford University Press is a department of the University of Oxford.
It furthers the University's objective of excellence in research, scholarship,
and education by publishing worldwide. Oxford is a registered trade
mark of Oxford University Press in the UK and in certain other countries

© Oxford University Press 2015

The moral rights of the author have been asserted

First published in 2015

2019

13

ISBN: 978 0 19 450217 7

Printed in China

This book is printed on paper from certified and well-managed sources

ACKNOWLEDGEMENTS

*The authors would like to thank all the teachers and students round the world whose
feedback has helped us to shape* English File.

The authors would also like to thank: all those at Oxford University Press (both
in Oxford and around the world) and the design team who have contributed
their skills and ideas to producing this course.

*Finally very special thanks from Clive to Maria Angeles, Lucia, and Eric, and from
Christina to Cristina, for all their support and encouragement. Christina would also like
to thank her children Joaquin, Marco, and Krysia for their constant inspiration.*

*The authors and publisher are grateful to those who have given permission to reproduce
the following extracts and adaptations of copyright material:* p.6 Extract from
"Ang Lee: My family values" by Elaine Lipworth, www.theguardian.com,
26 April 2013. Copyright Guardian News and Media Ltd 2013. Reproduced
by permission. p.9 Adapted extract from "'Best job in the world' took its toll
on tired Briton" by Bonnie Malkin, *The Telegraph*, 2 January 2010. © Telegraph
Media Group Limited 2010. Reproduced by permission. p.13 Adapted extract
from "Does Learning A New Language Give You A New Personality?" by Cody
Delistraty, http://thoughtcatalog.com, 18 November 2013. © 2015 The Thought
& Expression Co. All rights reserved. Reproduced by permission. p.16 Extract
from "Scientists pinpoint age when childhood memories fade" by Richard
Gray, www.telegraph.co.uk, 10 January 2014. © Telegraph Media Group
Limited 2014. Reproduced by permission. p.19 Adapted extract from "Revenge
Is Sweet" by Lindsay Clydesdale, *Daily Record*, 25 October 2006. Reproduced
by permission of Mirrorpix. p.29 Adapted extract from "How not to read" by
Lionel Shriver, www.theguardian.com, 8 February 2014. Copyright Guardian
News and Media Ltd 2014. Reproduced by permission. p.32 Adapted extract
from "Is being late fashionable or rude?" by Robert Rowland Smith, *The Sunday
Times*, 4 September 2011. Reproduced by permission of News UK & Ireland
Limited. p.35 Extract from "Does money make you happy?" by Stephen
Evans, www.bbc.co.uk, 6 April 2010. © BBC News Website. Reproduced
by permission. p.39 Adapted extract from "How long does it really take
to change a habit?" by Oliver Burkeman, *The Guardian*, 10 October 2009.
Copyright Guardian News and Media Ltd 2009. Reproduced by permission.
p.48 Adapted extract from "Matisse's cut-outs, review: 'a guaranteed winner'"
by Richard Dorment, *The Telegraph*, 15 April 2014. © Telegraph Media Group
Limited 2014. Reproduced by permission. p.52 Adapted extract from
"Homeopathy is no better than a placebo, scientists claim" by Kashmira
Gander, www.independent.co.uk , 9 April 2014. Reproduced by permission
of The Independent. p.58 Adapted extract from "You're never too old to have
a pet, especially if you feel lonely or ill" by Liz Gill, *The Times*, 2 September
2003. Reproduced by permission of News UK & Ireland Limited. p.61 Adapted
extract from "The Way We Eat Now", *The Times*, 20 April 2013. Reproduced
by permission of News UK & Ireland Limited. p.62 Adapted extract from "The
30-day worm and cricket diet" by Jason Caffrey, www.bbc.co.uk, 28 February
2015. © BBC News Website. Reproduced by permission. p.65 "Double Face",
from *The Joy Luck Club* by Amy Tan, copyright © 1989 by Amy Tan. Used by
permission of Abner Stein and G. p. Putnam's Sons, an imprint of Penguin
Publishing Group, a division of Penguin Random House LLC. p.68 Adapted
extract from "Michael Mosley: "Three minutes of exercise a week will keep
you fit"" by Jenni Murray, *Radio Times*, 28 February 2012. Reproduced by
permission of Barbara Levy Literacy Agency.

Sources: www.pipedown.info

Illustrations by: Atsushi Hara c/o Dutch Uncle Agency pp.4, 5, 12, 33, 43, Anna
Hymas c/o New Division Ltd p.14, Joanna Kerr p.59, Olivier Latyk c/o Good
Illustration Agency pp.19, 68, Roger Penwill pp.8, 11, 29, 37, 45, Tim Marrs
p.26

*The publisher would like to thank the following for their kind permission to reproduce
images*: Alamy Images pp.20 (spear/Valentyna Chukhlyebova), 23 (Terry
Deary/Mark Waugh), 27 (reading/Images of Birmingham Premium), 28 (The
Lord of the Rings/Ben Molyneux), 28 (The Hunger Games/Cristina Fumi),
35 (bank card/Paul Fleet), 35 (scratch card/David Lee), 38 (jogger/Tetra Images),
40 (access denied/Alex Stojanov), 48 (gallery/HelloWorld Images), 48 (Henri
Matisse/INTERFOTO), 50 (xray/Elisanth), 61 (roast dinner/Jack Hobhouse),
61 (sushi/David Pearson), 62 (insects on plate/Maximilian Weinzierl), 67 (twins/
Stuart Monk); Bridgeman Art Library Ltd/The Tretchikoff Project (Pty) Ltd
p.47, The Chinese Girl c.1950s (oil on canvas), © Tretchikoff, Vladimir (1913-
2006)/Private Collection); Corbis pp.25 (Evelyn Glennie/Mike Blake/Reuters),
29 (Lionel Shriver/Jenny Lewis); The Folio Society edition of The Handmaid's
Tale © Anna & Elena Balbusso 2012 c/o Shannon Associates p.49; Getty Images
pp.5 (children/Cultura/Judith Wagner Fotografie), 5 (girl playing/Jodie Griggs),
9 (Ben Southall/Torsten Blackwood/AFP), 15 (students/Steve Debenport),
31 (siblings/hero Images), 32 (waiting/Stephen Simpson), 34 (coins/JGI/
Jamie Grill), 39 (apples/Fred Dimmick), 58 (puppy/Life On White); Oxford
University Press p.13; Rex Features pp.6 (Ang Lee/), 21 (The Last Emperor 1987/
Columbia/Everett), 21 (Cate Blanchett/Moviestore), 25 (Evelyn Glennie/Fabio
De Paola), 28 (The Return of the King 2003/New Line/Everett), 28 (The Hunger
Games:Mockingjay Part 1); Shutterstock pp.10 (take your daughter to work
day/Stacey Newman), 16 (birthday party/Creativa Images), 20 (arrow/Andrey
Burmakin), 20 (bow and arrows/Christian Weber), 20 (bullet/Ziggylives),
20 (cannon/artkamalov), 20 (Greek helmet/Vartanov Anatoly), 20 (rifle/
Militarist), 20 (missile/Orion-v), 20 (Bronze shield/Tatiana Popova), 20 (sword/
oksana2010), 23 (Ancient Egyptian artwork/ksana-gribakina), 35 (banknotes/
ppart), 35 (lotto ticket/alexmillos), 36 (woman and dog/Zurijeta), 42 (phone/
patpitchaya), 50 (lemon & honey tea/Teresa Kasprzycka), 52 (pharmacy bottles/
Szasz-Fabian Ilka Erika), 55 (hiker/Warren Goldswain), 56 (snail/Eric Isselee),
63 (Castle Combe/JeniFoto); The Random House Group Limited p.65, Book
cover: The Joy Luck Club written by Amy Tan, artwork © Chris Corr, used by
arrangement with The Random House Group Limited

Designed by: Bryony Clark